Madame COURAGE

MARTIN KARI

Copyright © 2025 Martin Kari.

All rights reserved. No part of this book may be reproduced, stored, or transmitted by any means—whether auditory, graphic, mechanical, or electronic—without written permission of both publisher and author, except in the case of brief excerpts used in critical articles and reviews. Unauthorized reproduction of any part of this work is illegal and is punishable by law.

ISBN: 978-1-63950-364-3 (sc)
ISBN: 978-1-63950-365-0 (hc)
ISBN: 978-1-63950-366-7 (e)

Because of the dynamic nature of the Internet, any web addresses or links contained in this book may have changed since publication and may no longer be valid. The views expressed in this work are solely those of the author and do not necessarily reflect the views of the publisher, and the publisher hereby disclaims any responsibility for them.

Writers Apex

Gateway Towards Success

8063 MADISON AVE #1252
Indianapolis, IN 46227
+13176596889
www.writersapex.com

CONTENTS

Dedication v
Acknowledgements vii
About the Author ix
Notes xi
Back Cover Blurb xiii
Prologue xv

Chapter 1   The Journey Begins 1
Chapter 2   Early Childhood 10
Chapter 3   School Years in Turku and Nokia 28
Chapter 4   Going Away From Finland 70
Chapter 5   Priorities in Turku and Nokia 88
Chapter 6   Away From Finland: Meeting Martin 104
Chapter 7   Enrolment in Finland: Heidelberg/Germany ... 118
Chapter 8   Sweden – Germany – Finland / Engagement ... 129
Chapter 9   First Life Together in Germany 139
Chapter 10 Tying the 'Knot' 142
Chapter 11 Life Between Germany and Finland 153
Chapter 12 Life in South Africa 162
Chapter 13 Life in Brazil 166
Chapter 14 Excursion to Germany 175
Chapter 15 Calling Australia Home 178

Epilogue 187

DEDICATION

For Arja Kari—my wife, my partner, my Madam Courage

This book is for you, Arja.

From the day we met, your courage, warmth, and spirit shaped every step of my journey. You carried with you the light of Finland's birch forests, the strength of your family, and the boundless curiosity that led us across continents and through life's many trials.

You were never just beside me—you were my compass, my strength, my home. Your laughter softened the hardest days, your wisdom steadied every storm, and your love gave meaning to it all.

Though you are no longer here in this world, every page of this book holds your voice, your presence, your memory. It is a tribute to the extraordinary woman you were: a daughter, a mother, a friend, and above all, my wife—my Madam Courage.

This story belongs to you, Arja, as does my heart—always.

With eternal love,

Martin

ACKNOWLEDGEMENTS

I would especially like to thank Adam Salviani for his so important support. Special thanks again to my personal editor. Karen Mackay, who had the patience and great knowledge to guide me through this book. Last, but not least, I' am grateful for the assistance of my wife, Arja, who brought forth so many details of her life story.

ABOUT THE AUTHOR

Born during World War II in Transylvania, Martin Kari has lived a colourful and multifaceted life, starting as a refugee in Germany. Technical and then formal higher education prepared the author for a life of exploration, adventure, intellect and humanity. Having worked in, and lived on, four continents as a global citizen, Martin eventually settled in Australia with his wife and six children.

It was only in retirement that he found the time to become the prolific writer he is today.

NOTES

Some of the personal names included in this book have been changed, or only first names have been included, to protect the privacy of those concerned.

Personal statements in this book is a word-smithing of the author.

Authenticity is not to be scrutinized here to the last bone for it is a 'biographical novel' asking also for embellishing elements.

Facts however, have been presented to my best knowledge.

BACK COVER BLURB

Albert Einstein already discovered that: "Life is like riding a bicycle; to keep your balance you must keep moving."

Madam Courage is the story of Arja Kari, the author's wife and soul mate. Born in Finland, Arja's childhood was immersed in the love and succour of her extended family. From these experiences came the self-confidence and courage that allowed her to face the challenges of life. Arja's great thirst for knowledge about other countries and the fascinating people from these different societies began with her ever-growing list of childhood penfriends. Never overly interested in formal studies (except perhaps in languages), Arja's passion was for the school of life. It was while on one of these trips that Arja met one of her penfriends who was later to become her husband and partner in life. Together they then continued the adventure that is Madam Courage's life.

Summer birch forest - Finland

PROLOGUE

Madam Courage

How is courage born? Let me introduce to you, the reader, the simple truth that courage, like many other character traits, has a humble start in an individual's life. During life we are all on a journey on which courage has always been an essential companion. Some of us have courage; others have less of it, but we all need courage to make life's journey.

Here is essentially the first part of my wife's life-journey. During my own life, I learned to honour her as 'Madam Courage'. Her life before we met and her personal viewpoints are the subject of this book. This account highlights again that most of the time not only different personalities, but also different life paths have the power of attraction. Those differences can support a life together as long as both parties manage to step aside from an exclusively self-centred individual position so that a mutual learning process can, over time, take place. This is a vital rule in life, especially in cases where people come from very different backgrounds. In our case my wife, Arja, is from Finland and I am from Transylvania (Romania), *Dracula* country.

We all travel through life never knowing our destinies. As Emilie Carles once said, "There is however a novel in everybody's life, if only it could be written by everybody." Having written about my life before meeting Arja in Volume One of 'Journey of a Lifetime' and also about our lives together in Volume Two of the same title, I am simply honoured and humbled to write this book as well. The idea came from Pirkko and Kalevi, our Finnish friends who started this process with a comment, "Why not write about the life of Arja before you met."

This chapter in the life of my wife is earmarked by a stable, happy childhood starting in 1945 just before the end of World War II, and is quite different from mine - Martin, the husband and writer. A good childhood can be regarded as an asset for a successful adulthood. 'Madam Courage', Arja, went out with a personal strength to test this in the real world, meeting people from other cultures, often away from family and the security of home. Courage has been her constant companion on her journey with her own family of eight through four continents in an extraordinary life in which her steady courageous, non-fearful role took centre stage, mostly quiet, listening, and supportive in her Finnish *sisu* (steadfastness).

Now in 2009, after forty-two years 'bound' together, we have learned a bit more about each other, which should be a sound starting point for this biography. Why not continue working as a team in which one writes what the other wants to say. Here then is the result of what Arja, 'Madam Courage', has said and what I have put on paper to the best of my ability.

Typical Middle Finland

CHAPTER 1

The Journey Begins

The year 1944 became an eventful year also in Finland. The country in the north of Europe was engulfed in the Second World War with Russia (then the Soviet Union) as its primary antagonist. Only the determination of the Finnish people saved the independence of this small country from the mighty Russian military power. Neighbouring countries of Estonia, Latvia and Lithuania were not so successful at the time in defending their sovereignty against Russia. The meddling of the German military did not succeed in Finland and after a dubious German retreat, Finland courageously kept Russia out of the country. This valiant fight saved its sovereignty.

Approximately twenty-five years later in Germany, a relative of Martin's adoptive parents repeatedly told of his war experience in Finland. The story was always accompanied by the proud display of his brass medallion from the Finnish war. When Martin saw it, he immediately recognised it, and added, "I saw in the drawer of my father-in-law's desk a whole number of those war memorabilia." All of a sudden, the 'victorious battle medallion' turned out to be the only confirmation of his presence during the war in Finland. Arja, on the other hand, could not remember her father Petteri ever having mentioned a word of the war. Were they then the real war heroes?

The first time Petteri actually heard of Martin's existence and his relationship with Arja, he commented, "Rather a Russian than a German," meaning, a Russian was bad enough, but a German was even worse. However, it also needs to be said that time and personal encounters instantly changed Petteri's view. Many things in life depend on a personal touch.

During the difficult wartime, Finland also asked its devoted young female population to support the defense efforts of their men. The whole population of the country was once again unified in defending the country against the Goliath invader, Russia. Strength of unity was reflected in the support for each other. This did much to help ease a community suffering.

Winter far in the north of Europe has always been an extremely difficult time. When temperatures can drop below minus 40 degrees Celsius, it brought military action on the ground almost to a halt. This gave the Finns an advantage on their own territory. Russia found itself disadvantaged under such difficult conditions in the enemy's territory. The *Lotta-Svard* Organisation of Finland also sent its courageous women to assist war efforts by supplying food, clothes, first aid and intelligence. The *Lottas*, as they were called, were a chain of support from homes and towns into the fields and front lines. Tysse (Thyra) Elina Jarvi, hailing from a good family stock out of Pispala/Tampere in Middle Finland, was also one of these *lotta*s.

Family of Arja's mother – Tampere/Finland 1943

At the age of twenty-six, her charm and beauty didn't go unnoticed past the war frontlines. Only Petteri Kari could win Tysse's attention in the middle of the war. By any standards, he was a man of good appearance. However, he came with a less than convincing family background. Nevertheless, humans by nature are compensated eventually for shortfalls. On one side, Petteri had his good looks and his ability to show what a man of his calibre was worth. He never fell short of great phantasies, actions and above all, he knew how to play his role and achieve what he wanted.

Petteri could probably have turned out to be a great actor under different circumstances. However, at the time in 1944 his acting role continued with Tysse. The moment Petteri saw her, they both fell in love. During a war, the reality of harsh circumstances has always brought people together quicker because everybody lived in fear of losing his or a loved one's life. Beauty and strong appearance also may have brought Tysse and Petteri together quicker than it would have happened in peacetime. Uncertainty is a more common occurrence during war as different conditions bring on different outcomes.

Tysse and Petteri's wedding took place in the early days after meeting each other, as was the custom at that time. Commitment is still the basis for everything in our lives; we change this and we do not have to wonder why many problems take over in our lives. The parents of Tysse, who lived in Pispala near Tampere, wanted to be convinced that Petteri was a good husband for their daughter, who had lived all her life under the guidance of caring parents. Petteri, on the other hand, was more a man of the world, already in a rush to leave behind his previous colourful life. He begged on his knees in front of his future parents-in-law, "A good wife will also make me a good husband." Despite the theatrical scene, Tysse's mother, Army, and father, Artturi, gave their seal of approval to their marriage.

A marriage in those days was a family affair, reflecting on a mutual dependency and asking also for confirmation within the family. Possibly linked to the rise in living standards, - mainly in the Western World and only towards the turn of the first Millennium - this tradition of a family sanctioned marriage has experienced changes away from the family towards the more independent wishes of the bride and groom, remaining an open agreement between partners. Good times have traditionally caused the downfall of our human relations. Only difficult times restore our efforts for the better. Is that one reason why, in the beginning of the Second Millennium, so many marriage commitments have come only so far, not to last, but to dissolve so easily? It must be more than a family tradition to keep a marriage together as even the marriage of Tysse and Petteri did not last for a lifetime.

Mother Tysse – wedding photo -23.7.1944

As nothing in this world lasts forever, so it was with World War II. After such a measure of widespread ignorance, it was important for the ones who had survived to continue life in a better way. When all hope through war seemed to have evaporated, new life is often the best way back to normality. Shortly before the end of World War II, on 7th of April 1945, Tysse gave birth to her first daughter, Arja. She arrived two months premature, which couldn't be regarded too much out of order considering the war time was drawing closer to an end. Everything had come to an end at that time, but new beginnings couldn't wait in a victory for life to continue. Baby Arja, the 'actress' of this story, entered the world a little lighter than other babies, but with a determined will for a life in the Finnish southern city of Turku.

On the day of her birth, Arja's father, Petteri, was very upbeat, celebrating the event outside of the home in the company of his mate, Hessu. They celebrated with unlimited alcohol as if they were the 'creators' of this world. Apart from this, Tysse had the support of her parents, a support a young mother needs especially on her very first confinement. How is it that often men are 'overwhelmed' in the circumstances associated with a child's birth, despite women being the 'stars' of the birth? Petteri didn't stop short, giving the day its own motto, which lived on in many a family memory. April seventh was the day when Hessu and Petteri had their binge (*paiva huhtikuun oli seitsemas kun Hessu ja Petteri ryllas*).

Besides this, more pressing commitments had arrived for the parents with the birth of Arja. The tasks based around the new family member initially kept everybody united. War had left a legacy for everybody to seek support for new directions again closer to the family. Petteri finished the house, which lay on a property overlooking a Baltic Sea arm outside Turku, by himself over the years. The land climbed slightly uphill towards the house in an oblong garden, the road running behind it. Next to one side of the property, on the right side with the view from the house to the sea-arm below, huge granite boulders rose to a hill site covered only sparsely with the notorious pine and birch trees of the Finnish forest. Down on the beach between sea grass a wooden pier jutted out into the water where a rowing boat lay at anchor. The other side of the sea-arm was within reach for a good swimmer.

Tysse and Petteri

Across the sea arm, the city started with multi-storey flat blocks, going inland and facing north. In the far distance the solid stony historical square-built castle tower could be seen. Years later, to the west of the water, a bridge was built from Hirvensalo to the city. At the time though, everybody used a boat service to get across. The whole southwest of Finland is cut into many sea-arms with thousands of rocky islands on which the Finnish forest incessantly strives against nature's fury during cold and long winters.

Back on the property, a separate sauna building was added, not far from the water. As time passed, the garden leading to the house mainly sheltered rows of low trimmed hedges along a central footpath with paths going off to both sides. Scattered here and there was a veggie patch or one of the few fruit trees that managed to grow on the mainly rocky, granite ground. The house entrance started level with the upper road, allowing, amidst the first drop of the terrain, a rock wall to raise the first floor from the garden. Glass windows of the later closed-in veranda, extended life inside the house throughout the year with views onto the garden, even during the bitterly cold winter. Bay windows on each side overlooked the whole garden side.

In the summer the windows could be left open in a secured position, bringing the warmth and light into the house. There was also a large living room and three bedrooms, of which one was solely for Arja, but was shared three years later with her sister Raija. Further on near the entrance was the kitchen and a corridor leading to each room through the house. The inside of the house was renovated over time, in natural timber, giving the necessary isolation and cosy atmosphere as well. An advanced centralised heating system supplied, from the ground level, cosy heat throughout the whole house during the long, cold months of the year. Bad summer years sometimes called for continued heating with coal briquettes or timber, whatever was available.

These memories of the home in Honkaistenranta only help to support its own history. Nothing was ever finished quickly, as everything required its own time, as it still does today, to develop into something that we can fondly remember. And so it was with the home in Honkaistenranta. Only years after father Petteri had started, did it reach a status, which could have been called a finished home. The family though happily lived in it from early on, expanding the living area as much as progress with the house allowed.

Tysse with Arja, 1946

On a separate note, Arja had early fond memories of her home. One was a visit of friends who brought along as a home-warming gift something special, namely some oranges. What a surprise! When shown how to peel the orange, she found inside a living worm. It was only with some assurances that Arja could be moved to try the orange after its 'inmate' was removed – her first orange-experience.

An episode that saved Arja's young life occurred during the first years on the Honkaistenranta property. For a number of years regularly during summer months, a family lived in the cottage further down in the garden, paying a modest rent to supplement the family income. Their two children, Anneli and Jukka, were great playmates during that time. One day while playing, Arja fell off the pier straight into the water. At the age of three, she couldn't swim at all yet. Luckily, the other girl, Anneli was older and could grab Arja's long hair, which floated on top of the surface. She pulled Arja's head out from under the water while Jukka, her brother, rushed to the house calling for help. Arja narrowly escaped drowning that time. Luck has always been one of life's companions!

The house was sold in 1964. It was to be seventeen years later, on a homecoming visit to Finland in 1981, before Arja saw her early home again. The Honkaistenranta property with the house had been neglected and run down. On the next visit in 1992 though, the new owners, an architect couple, were about to restore the property. They wanted to rebuild it, not just to its past glory, but considerably improving on it and returning it more or less to the status of Arja's childhood. In coming years, a later visit confirmed the rejuvenation of a childhood dream. We are also connected to our past more than we are prepared to admit. A home, even when it changes hands, can still recall past memories of our lives. Moreover, when these memories remain positive, they can become much better ones.

CHAPTER 2

Early Childhood

Honkaisteranta, family home, Turku-Finland, 1955

This home was the family castle, holding an abundance of good memories. Daily life paralleled the immediate needs of a post-war era. Father Petteri was a jack-of-all-trades, not only doing everything by himself, but also always finding what was needed. There was never any real shortage of food with plenty on the table - fish from the sea, potatoes, the brown Finnish hole-bread (one of the many Finnish bread varieties), butter, milk, meat, and in summer a selection of fresh veggies out of the garden supplemented supplies as did blueberries and cranberries from the forest. Strawberries came on the market only in later years while in winter, preserved pickled cucumber or cabbage was always on the menu.

A strong man like father Petteri was never short of his beer despite, in post-war years in Finland, alcohol being only available on strictly regulated alcohol cards (*viinakortti*). The outlets were also kept to a strict minimum so that in the remote northern parts of Finland, one store in Rovaniemi served, for instance, an area of hundreds of kilometres. No wonder the liquor store turned into a 'Mecca' for many Finns, because whatever is strictly limited, usually gains in importance.

Unlike Arja's childhood, whenever Finland went through difficult times in the past, food was an issue. Six hundred years of Swedish rule followed one hundred and eight years by Russia. In 1917, Finland gained its independence and the Finnish people have remained one nation, upholding their very own language and culture against near impossible odds. The Nobel Prize Laureate Frans Emil Sillanpaa also describes in his prize winning novel 'Silja, the maid' ('Nuorena Nukkunut') the difficult times experienced by the people, especially in the country. There were times when people had nothing to eat, particularly during unforgivingly harsh winters. Flour was mixed then with finely crushed pine bark while during summer, stinging nettles and dandelions made up for a variety in food. When the flour ran out, pine bark helped fill hungry bellies and stopped the stomach rumbling.

Disposable nappies for babies were also unknown. Even after the end of World War II, times were difficult. Mothers of large families had to look after their children and make sure they did not run outside during the severely cold winter. From stories told out of remote eastern parts of Finland, Karelija (Karjala), children sometimes ended up with chilblains marked on their buttocks for the rest of their lives.

Difficult times have always required special measures, often resulting in unconventional results. Father Petteri, however, knew how to make the 'bobs' for a living with everything that came along, whether it was a trucking business, boat building, sand mining, and all sorts of racketeering. Activities often kept Petteri away from home for long periods so that the housework was mainly left to mother Tysse. That included raising Arja and her younger sister Raija, three years her junior.

Arja and sister Raija, 1948

Arja's grandparents came on regular visits from Tampere, either around mid-summer, at the end of June or at Christmas time. On one of their summer visits, sometime in 1945, shortly after the birth of Arja, her mother and grandmother wanted to visit a local cinema. The men were given the task of looking after the baby. Petteri had his hands full looking after his baby daughter and not really knowing what to do with her, especially when she unmistakably made the point of missing her mum. During the course of this evening, Petteri suffered enough listening to articulated noises so that he completely forgot about a nappy change, which most likely further upset the baby.

When the movie party returned home, only two people were happy - father Petteri and grandfather Artturi. What was soon discovered was the cause of the baby's very loud voice - the textile nappies couldn't hold everything anymore and when the mess found its way up through the neck of the baby's clothes, the men had no explanation for this appearance. Tysse and her mother did though, but instead of showing disappointment with the men's efforts, put all hands on to free the baby from the mess. The occasion made two nicknames stick for many years to come - 'beer pants' (*kaljapoksy*) and 'tutti frutti' for Arja to try everything out. Petteri disappeared from the scene as quickly as he could, leaving the clean up to the 'professionals'. How good are men when it comes to raising children? Isn't there a common saying, "To become a father is easy, but to be a father difficult."

Father Petteri also had his stronger sides, which didn't always fit easily into family life. He must have had a barrel-like stomach. He could proudly tell everybody that he never got drunk, despite regularly testing with his mates who could gulp as much as possible of the 'liquid bread' down and stay sober. Those exercises took place after a day's work, lasting too often all night and ultimately upsetting the daily routine in the family home.

The 'hero' often needed the daytime in order to catch up with his missing sleep. Tysse kept these disturbances to herself, keeping up home blessings so that Arja and Raija could experience an unspoiled childhood. *Aiti*, as mum is called in Finnish, began to have sleepless nights when Petteri was away from home. Over the years, this affected her health so that she could hardly find sleep at all anymore. The force of habit often drives our lives. Yet she never complained or lost her bright outlook on life always keeping her cheerfulness.

Tysse and Petteri, 1956

Tysse wanted to pass on to her children the experience of a good family life similar to her own childhood experiences. Fortunately, she could also bank on the support of friends. In the neighbourhood lived a couple, Signe and Into, who frequently helped out, looking after the two girls so that Tysse could find time now and then for a much needed rest.

In return, Tysse didn't hesitate to help someone else when needed. In the neighbourhood, a boy called Kullervo was born in the same year as Arja. Following his early adoption, the new mother had difficulties bringing him up because no baby formula was available at that time. Luckily, mother Tysse had plenty of milk to help out and therefore more or less saved Kullervo's life in those difficult times. Was it the same mother's milk that drew Kullervo to Arja with whom she wanted nothing to do? For many years to come Arja didn't want to know anything about the opposite sex because of the example of her father.

She was determined never to get married. It was much later in her life that a 'circuit breaker' arrived to change her mind.

The friendship with Signe went on for a very long time; even past the life expectation of Tysse's 85 years. More than sixty years later from the beginning of this neighbourly friendship, Arja has kept in touch with Signe throughout her life. On special occasions like Signe's 100th birthday in 2008, Arja called her by phone from Australia. Australia had become the destiny of Arja's family's life-journey. In hindsight, she had a happy childhood. Finland was a good and steady home. It was only after childhood that something enticed Arja out into the world. The home atmosphere seemed to have become too narrow. The personal freedom that resulted must have looked for life's challenges.

The days went peacefully by. The family had everything it needed and generally people were not in each other's way thanks to the relatively small population Finland had and still has up to the present time. People did not have to compete as much for a living space, which resulted in closer relationships between people, at least at the time. Aspirations to raise living standards have, over the years, distanced people in Finland somewhat by competing for a more consumer based lifestyle. However, during Arja's early childhood, life remained mostly steady, as everybody was preoccupied with the little that war had left behind.

Tysse with Arja and Raija, Honkaisteranta, 1956

Two of these things was the sandpit in the garden and a timber cubby house Petteri had built for Arja and her sister Raija. Also, under mother Tysse's watchful eyes, both girls learned to swim early in the shallow sea water adjacent to the property. There were ball games with the kids in the neighbourhood. It was never boring. There were sibling quarrels, but mum's care always kept them in check.

Later in life it became quite obvious how different the sisters were from each other. While Arja might have developed into a more solitary person, Raija became the opposite, a busybody. No wonder their lives followed very different pathways. Arja saw the world during her life, whereas her sister remained in Finland going through the changes of her life in the one place she had always called home.

When Petteri was at home, he made up for lost time by playing the best imaginable 'good-time-uncle'. His own fairytales and adventure stories fascinated everybody, including the neighbours' children, who stayed on far into the night to experience the fairytale world. Petteri could produce by his magic. Actually he managed this way from time to time to make up lost ground with his family. It is a pity that the details of his stories were lost because it would have made a fantastic children's fairytale collection - one in which Petteri was also a great actor.

Today Arja can recall only one of her father's goodnight stories, which has remained especially in her memory - a story told of how young stowaways came to see the world with its many different, marvellous countries unnoticed and free of charge. The following morning this prompted two friends from the neighbourhood to 'pilgrim' all the way to the harbour, where the police, already alerted by the parents, picked them up near a docked ship fortunately just in time before the kids' plan to secretly board a ship could turn into reality. Once the two arrived in front of the monstrous hull, they couldn't pluck up the courage any more to board the 'monster'. In the end, a return home for the two runaways was not quite so distant and adventurous any more in the care of the police. How easily an idea can sometimes spark action, regardless of age and especially when phantasies lack the experience of much needed reality. When the end turns out well, nothing is lost, even in a young dreamers' excursion. Nobody in the neighbourhood could therefore be upset when the police returned the two 'world travellers' safely to their doorsteps. On hearing about the incident, Petteri was amused, promising that from then on he would try to tell less adventurous goodnight stories.

The fact is that where there is much sunshine, there is also a lot of shade. This had been the case with Petteri too. Life doesn't always run on an even keel, allowing only the good to dominate. Children adored Petteri for he was a gentle, strong personality, showing it unfortunately more outside of his own family than on the home front. Home was, for Petteri, a place of refuge, which he sought when he needed it. Sometimes he seemed to have no limits to his self-assurance, but insiders like his own wife could see through this veneer. When Petteri had money, nothing stopped him from playing the greatest actor, but lack of money turned him into a surprisingly, quiet person trying to get away from himself.

Dressing up, Tysse and Petteri with friends

It was not difficult to establish in which 'reality' Petteri was standing at any one time. One day, reports reached the family home that Petteri had staged his own show, making flying objects out of current bank notes and throwing them to passing pedestrians from a shop entrance, not hesitating to also fulfil individual customer's wishes from inside the shop. No wonder Petteri was regarded the hero of the day as everybody around him was happy about such a performance, including Petteri. Listening to what people had to say about this extravagancy, mother Tysse on the other hand definitely was not impressed, as this giveaway money would have better served the family.

Anyway, special people like Petteri couldn't be measured by normal standards. Arja later came to know that Petteri's mother had spoiled him too much in comparison to his older brother. Such inconsistency in raising children during the difficult times after World War I led to extreme behaviour patterns - the neglected brother ended up hanging himself, while the spoilt son, Petteri, could never get enough recognition in life. Both brothers channelled their controversial early lives into contentious adulthood.

Everybody's life is like a building. The building blocks really matter and how they are put in place in order to form a proper building - a home with relative stability – is basically the same for everyone. When the foundation begins shakily, the rest that follows is likely to be shaky as well. Only a person with outstanding self-discipline can go back to the foundation to make corrections. Petteri had many outstanding character features, but he had a definite shortcomings in self-discipline.

Another attraction was soon on Petteri's timetable. He had organized, God knows from where, a tank from the war and put it back on the street one day. Firstly though, he put lots of children in it and together they had a great time driving through the city and stopping all the traffic. In the end, police stopped this fun drive only after people across the whole city centre had taken note of this extraordinary event. If the children were not in the tank, most people would probably have thought that war had started again, such was the confusion amongst most ordinary citizens. Petteri still managed to focus on the bright side of the event and not let the others spoil the fun. He was the one who started it and knew also how to get out of it unharmed. Having been a known personality to almost everybody in and around town, he certainly also benefited from his public status in which 'mates do not harm mates'. When somebody wanted to challenge him, he was never at a loss.

On another day, a little rogue out of the neighbourhood had the audacity to argue with Petteri about whether or not somebody would have the courage to smear tar onto their face. As this challenge didn't abate, Petteri went off to grab some tar from his workshop, returning to the scene and showing that he could do what was asked for. A big stink from the neighbours followed, but the storm disappeared again as quickly as it had arrived. Who would stand up in front of Petteri?

All in all, father Petteri definitely was a man of his own class! Virtually nothing could stop him from proving this to himself. Fortunately, mother Tysse understood how to keep the 'garbage' out of family life, especially when it came to undertakings, which Petteri knew to justify with, "I am ahead of my time". Other women often gave him a helping hand, which should not be a complete surprise, considering his strong appearance and very good looks.

At a certain time, Petteri couldn't get a business with women off the ground, all the while trying to receive the secret approval. This venture got nowhere because in Finland the law doesn't allow, even today, 'the commercial exploitation of women'. This kind of enterprise only became noticeable later when mother Tysse spoke for the first time about life-sized pin-up girls, which had decorated the room of the newlyweds in the house of Petteri's mother. As a child, Arja could not understand this sort of behaviour, but experienced instead a personal confusion, which continued to haunt her for many years to come.

There was on one side the feeling that Arja should grow into a good woman; on the other was the example of Petteri, sending mixed messages about women. At the same time out of this milieu, Arja and her sister were probably the first in the whole country to receive a wonderful, rubber Donald Duck and a beautiful, big walking doll from Sweden. They were both much admired and the Donald Duck managed to still be with Arja in Australia, 60 years later.

Mother Tysse spoke every now and then about Petteri's extravagances with other women in order to protect her own family. She got caught between the fronts while her main goal remained however to raise, in the best possible way, her two children with the help of family and friends. Her personal pride as a woman of outstanding character and appearance overlooked for some time the negative fallout of an extraordinary husband. She could look past the problems into the future of her two children, managing also to keep everybody around her, including her own family, on positive terms with life and the negative sides away from others.

She must have thought, "Nobody can turn these negative sides away, not to mention doing anything about it, so why should I bother other people?" This outright, courageous attitude was not without effect on her own well-being!

From early childhood, Arja kept mostly to herself, but was never incapable of occupying herself. Tysse came one day with a girl of the same age as Arja. At that time Tuija was also two years old and came from the neighbourhood, a little bit further away. Tysse and Tuija's mother, Sirkka, became friends simply out of the circumstances that both women had to deal with extraordinary husbands. The problems brought them closer.

While Petteri lived a life in full swing, rarely missing out on anything (good or bad), Arja's new friend's father frequently got into trouble for activities he couldn't always control. As a matter of fact, the mother of Tuija also had two girls and was constantly finding herself on the receiving end of trouble. The most disturbing part of it was that both mothers came from good family stock and had their hands full raising children in good faith away from the darker side of their husbands' lives. Petteri, however, was never caught *in flagrante*.

Tuija immediately became Arja's friend and remained friends throughout their whole lives. She had a very pleasant nature, always remaining happy and friendly. Her lips never said a bad word. Throughout her life, the question could be raised, "How come this person with such a positive outlook on life is continuously dealt such heavy blows throughout her life?" Does life follow preset conditions of good and bad? It is difficult to believe somebody can survive such conditions. While she never changed her friendly and open nature, her husband also went off the tracks, succumbing finally to a health problem.

Her only son followed most promisingly in the footsteps of his mother and led a healthy, steady life, but still tragedy caught up with him. He passed away far too early at the age of thirty, succumbing to cancer. This not being enough, friend Tuija who had lived an unparalleled, steady life, also passed away much too early at the age of sixty from cancer. The fate of Tuija might have had some connection to the nuclear accident of Chernobyl in the Soviet Union. The radiation fallout carried as far as Finland. Some people seem to get all the bad things in life, while others often disregard steady life rules and get away with it. Sensitivities of people unfortunately react differently to such unnatural exposure.

During childhood, Arja and Tuija stored up a vast number of happy memories. There were never any disagreements with time together spent always in an easy understanding in which neither of the girls ever tried to get the upper hand. As soon as school had taught them enough of how to read and write, they both spent time in enthusiastic reading, often exchanging fantasies from the stories and even staging plays, often held in Arja's garden. Other children loved to join in these plays as co-actors or spectators.

The best time in Finland has always been summer, when the days extend through the night with the sun only dipping below the horizon for a few hours. Nature's preparation for summer and its exodus into winter are short, distinct times of the year. Winter with its on and off time can extend up to nine months of the year. No wonder that everybody in Finland lives summer to the fullest.

During the month of May, virtually overnight, Finnish nature explodes into life with fresh, green colours. It is a show of nature's strength after a bitterly cold, long winter. During a good summer, the long sunny days last well into the night hours nearly to midnight and the sun returns in the first, early hours of the day. This happens everywhere except in the far north where the sun doesn't disappear at all. The longest day in the northern hemisphere, 21st of June, is a time of festivity when almost all Finns celebrate 'Mid-Summer Night' by ancient rituals of big bonfires and a good feast.

Storms during summer happened regardless of whether or not father Petteri was at home. Regular summer storms affected the family as Arja's mother and younger sister sought refuge each time with the neighbours in the hope of finding distraction from their fear in the company of others. According to them, talking to somebody behind thoroughly shut windows helped to focus their attention away from the intense lightning and its following rumbling that sent vibration waves through the air right into the house. In the case of none of the surrounding neighbours being at home, Tysse and Raija locked themselves into the bedroom hiding under the blanket. They buried their heads under pillows, wishing and hoping the thunder would go away to where they couldn't hear or see it.

Arja, on the other hand, stood on the other side laughing at them and saying, "There is nothing to worry about, the thunder is not after us in particular." She had no fear whatsoever because she knew that it would go again as quickly as it had arrived. At least the dog joined her in her room, reassuring himself by staying either close to Arja's side when she was sitting in front of her study desk or hiding under the bed.

Why worry about something we can't control anyway? Take it as it comes and remain watchful to do the right thing in case something unpredictable happens. The right thing would still be, to stay calm. Following this rule, we are also less likely to make mistakes. Tysse, however, could not be convinced to stay calm during a thunderstorm and wait through it, keeping some mental distance from the storm. This was one particular difference between mother and daughter. However, once the storm had gone, life continued once more along its usual path, eventually taking its course again more to everybody's likings. We all have stronger and weaker expressions, largely depending on how we look at life. All that matters in the end is that life continues.

Summer was the same for everybody - a time for outdoor living, compensating for the long, cold, twilight, winter days. Swimming was almost daily on the calendar and later when Arja became strong enough to row a boat further out into the sea-arm, hours were spent on the water. All this represented entertainment, which was offered then. Dogs in the family played their own role, but it was mainly Arja who spent time with the dogs because of her love of animals. During those days of her youth, dog Slipi, a lakeland terrier, often took his place on the highest point of the keel while he watched the pair of oars moving simultaneously, each one resting in a folk on the sides of the wooden boat on the rail approximately in the boat's centre. Slipi kept himself busy looking for fish, which sent air bubbles to the water's surface.

Not many other boats were on the water at these times as this archipelago of sea-arms spread over a vast area of the south-west coast of Finland, leaving more than enough spaces for the bigger boats to move further out. On sunny days, the seawater lay mostly calm, almost dark black between shores of mixed forest of dark green pine, light green leafy larches, spotted in between with birch trees of which the grey-white trunks stood out. Reddish timber houses often look from granite boulders through to the sea, whereas the smaller timber sauna buildings lined the shore.

Sauna is a Finnish cultural element carried along through history wherever the Finns moved on their migratory paths to today's Finland. During the week, apart from weekends, time could probably allow once more a sauna heater to get started, at that time with timber. A swim in the sea could alternately follow after a good hot sweat in the closed, heated sauna hut. A sauna visit delivers with its hot vapour the very best cleansing to the entire body. Even during winter, when the sea is frozen solid, many Finns dig ice holes and swim after a sauna in icy water, or roll in a snowfield. After such 'torture' everybody feels like a newborn; at least one will know by then to be healthy when surviving it. Especially after sauna, food and drinks are excellent companions in any party with friends or family.

Tysse, winter swim in ice hole

Returning from a pleasant, timeless, non pressing afternoon boat trip, it was essential to look after the dogs in order to keep them near the house. The dog before Slipi, Roy, a German long-coat pointer, caused neighbours to file complaints many times about their missing cats. In order to keep the peace, considerable amounts of money changed hands as lost pets suddenly rated extraordinarily high in value. However, neighbours didn't always necessarily seek to see somebody on the property about a lost cat or a chook. Once, a neighbour decided that she had had enough from the dog killing cats and called the police. This caused a great deal of anxiety over whether or not the dog would survive.

Another neighbour came to the rescue trying to find a way out of this sudden impasse, but she kept insisting, "This dog is now only for the police!" Roy was eventually taken away by the police. Later in the day, when Petteri turned up at home for a change, he answered the police request to appear in person. Petteri returned home sometimes later, miraculously bringing the dog back - to the anger of this certain neighbour. Petteri never mentioned how the dog was saved from being put down.

On another occasion, the dog Roy deposited a chook on the doorstep. While the dog was not sure as to whether he would receive approval or reprimand, he kept his foot across the chicken, preventing it from moving again. When somebody arrived to rescue the chook, the poor bird was already stripped of its feathers, but was still able to lay eggs, one of which the dog had firmly secured under his other front paw. Miracles do happen; the chook survived its ordeal! Not so much the egg, but the chook incident once more required the expert diplomacy father Petteri brought up with the neighbours. Admission, apology, determination with strong arguments were mixed in a way that Petteri always helped smooth the initial upset.

"Here we are again. We've got trouble but luckily you didn't lose the chook; so what can we do? To call the police, means only more trouble. I wouldn't rest before this is sorted out acceptably also for both of us. Let's find a way out for both of us and remain good neighbours. We will look after the dog better and you after your chook in future. Here take this consolation and we remain good neighbours. I don't want to hear anything anymore after we have departed. All I can offer you in addition is, come and we'll have a beer together to forget this regrettable event. We can't become cross with each other only because of a chook. Don't you think so? Come into my house and let's forget about all this."

At least for the sake of a good neighbourhood, the price was not too high in the end. After each summer, winter had to follow. First a short autumn set in, changing, sometimes only for one day, the leafy trees into a colourful display ranging from yellow to a variety of red. Even in the dying moments, nature displays its strength in a beauty, as if a farewell was meant only to be limited in order to become resurrected in a distant future. When during '*ruska*' (autumn leaf-change), the colourful leaves have fallen to the ground, the trees look empty; a skeleton of their branches is left behind.

Snow competing with the white of birch trees

Wind and rain gradually turn colder over the coming weeks until in late November, snow lightens the country from grey obscurity. Fields of rolling hills between forests have been harvested and the soil rests ploughed under a white layer of snow. The whole country has turned calm waiting for new life to return in a new edition and even waves were immobilized in the Baltic Sea by a growing ice-cover. This is then the time of life spent mainly inside houses where double windows and double outside-doors keep winter from penetrating homes. Busy ovens burn firewood, collected during summer and cut into regular sizes, spreading cosy warmth in Finnish homes during long winter months.

CHAPTER 3

School Years in Turku and Nokia

As soon as school started, reading became a preoccupation for Arja, one that served her well, especially during the long winters. It could almost be stated that when others fell short in the reading department, Arja made up for the shortfall.

Primary class II, Turku-Finland, 1954

On one of these occasions, when her grandparents and aunt from Tampere in Middle Finland came on their regular Christmas visit, they also brought along the book, *Lassie Come Home* by Erich Knight. Arja made an instant connection to the book, which at first glance was a story of a dog. While absorbed in the book Arja settled in, forgetting about everybody else. It was only after some time that the others realized she was missing. In fact, she was not so much missing, but on the contrary, everybody else had moved away, leaving her totally engrossed in the story of Lassie.

Books became a reliable partner carrying Arja through her entire life. During later years, when raising her own family of six children, time for books was not so readily available. Life's priorities meant books had to be set-aside for quite a number of years until her husband Martin took on writing during his retirement. This meant the return of the opportunity to actively read books in three different languages - English, Finnish, and German - but it also enabled Arja to act as an amateur editor and pre-polish Martin's writings.

Thus it was that Martin and Arja came to discover a worthwhile, new, common occupation. Attentive reading and writing can help unleash one's own spark of ideas, supported by creative images of fantasy. Whereas television, cinema, and video all produce finished images, a different world is created in the pages of a book. It became a whole life experience for Arja to prepare part of her life with experiences collected from books and then go out together with her husband Martin to collect real life experiences from many parts of the world.

Good life preparations have always helped to get through bad times that often in hindsight are recognized as some of the best ones. It is a good way to step aside in a life from time to time and escape from life's pressure, often coming from an early journey through the world of books.

Arja's mother Tysse realized this and supported her hobby in order to keep her isolated from the problems that father Petteri brought into the family. However, not everything was bad, but Tysse still managed to keep those potentially damaging and unnecessary experiences separate from those young lives. This earned her a lasting respect. Arja's younger sister led her life quite differently after she had grown up. Life's destiny probably ensured that Arja became closer to her grandparents and aunt whereas her sister was closer to her parents.

Arja and sister Raija. 1958

Arja's sister Raija already joined friends playing away from home whereas Arja found more freedom at home with her books and with excursions with the dog through the nearby fields and forests. There was also the company of long time friend Tuija, with whom Arja spent every available hour before her family moved to the city. They were both rather quiet young girls, sharing similar interests.

"The other kids in the neighbourhood quickly found a nickname for me," remembers Arja. "They called me 'sausage' because in their view I was too often *engrossed with my books. In their imagination all my reading could have turned me, eventually, into an idle sausage-like person. What they didn't always see was that I also had my share of activities at home with some work needing to be done inside and around the house. I had my small section of veggie garden, which was proudly maintained, so when a salad plant, carrot or onion came on the table out of the garden, the product of your own efforts tasted much better than the bought stuff."*

Besides all this, swimming, boating and trying to catch fish with very basic fishing gear, excursions to the city or into the surroundings and regular sauna helped to keep everybody busy enough. The other kids couldn't yet realize that they were rather the ones on the 'sausage' track. Life in the years ahead, actually confirmed that.

Going every so often by train to Tampere and staying for a week or so with her grandparents in Middle Finland was seen as a great personal privilege. Grandparents always had the time that one's own parents could hardly find. This generation's outlook on life, with their ample experience, can be beneficial for an upcoming generation. It enables them to look beyond present problems into the future.

'Mummi' and 'taata' (grandma and grandpa) had, on the ground floor of their house, their own grocery store at that time. The house lay on a busy road leading in and out of the city so that a great number of regular customers from around the area knew Arja's grandparents well. Their reliable service to shop visitors earned them a respected reputation. This was reflected by a steady flow of visitors during the day's opening hours without the so often unwanted interruptions of passing trade with which larger places in the city had to deal.

The day started very early here, especially when receiving the milk cans and the ice from the iceman. By the time Arja got out of her bed on the second floor in the front of the house, work in the shop had already been going for some hours during the very early morning.

Grandma and grandpa regularly changed the attendance in the shop so that most of the time there was somebody who had time for Arja. She also enjoyed her time in the shop, getting to know a number of people from the area. In return, they learned that she came from 'down south' in Turku. Here, in her grandparents' home, more people crossed Arja's life than at home outside the city of Turku. This must have had a bearing on the decision to move her, after the first basic school classes, from Turku to Tampere to live with her grandparents and aunt. Aune, her mother's sister, had also lived for most of her life in the house on the 'Pispalanvaltatie' number 59 (pispala-road).

Tampere was similar to home, further south in Turku. The Finnish landscape with its predominantly green pine forests, lakes, and fields came right up to the back door of the grandparents' house. Protruding boulders had been smoothened throughout prehistoric ice ages and could be seen up to where a small garden dropped down over the rocky outcrops.

The city with its suburbs is situated on a spit of land between two major inland lakes, Pyha Lake to the north and Nassy Lake to the south. 'Pyynikki' rises in the centre to a respectable hill site. Here, from a massive stone-set tower over the treetops, the eye can search the city across the lake surfaces on both sides into an endlessly green forest carpet, which borders the lakeshores.

Tampere was always known as the industrial hub of Finland with a strong presence of textile and paper manufacturing. Turku, on the other hand, prevailed as the historic cultural city. Constant rivalry traditionally emerges between the two cities in which Tampere boasts of its progress, while Turku claims to be the cradle of culture. A torrent of words has been exchanged between the cities throughout time. Turku has taunted, "Tampere has only one street, nothing else." In response, Tampere returns, "Turku has only 'kakola' (a prison) and 'samppalinna' (a good restaurant). If Turku is the cradle of culture, it's only because its culture is still in the cradle."

Turku-Castle, Southwest Finland

Apart from these amusing exchanges, both cities have, in real terms, something of their own to offer. When Turku claims ownership of culture, Tampere can also point to its great sons of literature. The carpenter/poet Laura Viita (born 1916) lived in Pispala, the home of Arja's grandparents.

On top of Pyynikki Hill, an artistic expression in metal can be found bearing the memory of its famous son. Not far from Tampere, in Hameenkyro, a picturesque lake forest area, the Nobel Prize Laureate Frans Emil Sillanpaa grew up (his prize winning work, 'Silja the maid').

Besides those cultural attributes, Tampere is a rich industrial city, which installed a world-first, rotating, outdoor summer theatre in Pyynikki. This bore tremendous attraction for Arja during her time in Tampere. During the later school years, Arja also visited Nokia, not far from Tampere. Nokia, which is the birthplace of today's electronic giant 'Nokia', was, in the early 1950s, a small place in an idyllic country site along a lake district in the middle of fir and birch forests. On the other hand, beech and oak trees were only found in the very south of the country near the Baltic Sea coast. This was because of the increasingly severe winter conditions, the further north Finland stretches.

Interestingly, in those early days, the company Nokia, which adopted the name from its location in the small town of Nokia, originally produced gumboots and car tires. It was only in the late 1960s that Nokia moved its production from gumboots to electronics. Their path was set with their invention of the first mobile phone. The very first mobile phone, in 1982, could hardly be carried because of its size and weight. At a legendary 15 kg and a price of 25000 Fin Mark, it still managed to start the revolution of mobile phone technology.

Nokia proved also to be a starting point for Arja, mostly because of its school. After a memorable, mainly quiet break with the grandparents in Tampere, life back in Turku seemed each time to have been better, at least for a short time. In these early times, Arja was torn between Turku and Tampere. Each time she changed location, she realised on reflection that everything looked different all of a sudden, to what it had appeared in close contact. However, her grandparents and Aunt Aune won her over a little bit more each time and influenced the decision to one day move to them.

During her first school years, near their home outside Turku, Arja met school requirements, but with no great enthusiasm. At that time, Finland still had primary and secondary education, which in later years changed into a universal single school system. This ensured everybody experienced education to the level that corresponded best to each individual's capabilities. Other countries, mainly in Europe, slowly moved to adopt this one-stream public education system. This was recognized internationally as the best service delivery for education, as more equal opportunities were given from the start.

Arja's lack of enthusiasm at school had nothing to do with the system. She was probably prepared somewhat earlier than most to live a more independent life, compared to the streamlined teaching methods that asked everybody to follow the rules collectively. Teachers in the

1950s applied strong discipline in all classes, very different to what is currently around at schools in 2009.

How good the system and the teachers were then can best be judged in hindsight with the individual's progress in life. Of course, everybody had his or her share of ups and downs during school life. Not all teachers reached the goal of becoming a good teacher and sometimes children responded with pranks. It was up to the individual teachers to control or correct this behaviour. Some teachers took their assignment seriously to the degree of producing their own show when the class began disturbing a lesson.

Arja remembers one female teacher for instance - surprisingly not the religion teacher - erupting one day into a desperate outburst. She had reached the point in her teaching when she was seeking refuge in a 'higher authority' for reasons probably related not only to her class. "Who doesn't believe in God, should leave the classroom immediately." The result was, most in the class laughed, ignoring the teacher, because nobody wanted to become the scapegoat in front of everybody.

Respect for the teacher could not have changed this way. Rather it was put on hold, not winning over the attention and respect of her students. Many children were not sheep-like followers, but generally speaking, most behaved within the rules. Some people seem to have picked a profession for which they were not fit enough to perform satisfactorily on a daily basis.

General observation leads to the conclusion that there were teachers with the right authority to run their lessons with discipline, while a few of them created their own problems in trying to lead a class of young, emerging characters. There have always been the good; as well the less good artisans, 'workmen' and teachers are no exemption. In real terms, it has always been like this and it will probably not change. A new generation always impatiently awaits their role in life, including their school years. Mutual respect in classes was still the norm for most school attendees.

"School discipline was already a challenge in my time," Arja recalls. "We were no angels, but usually it was just a small number of students who fooled around. One day outside the school premises during a lunch break, two male students calmly pulled a cigarette out and started to puff away, as adults tended to do in the company of some other students. My friend and I saw a female teacher coming our way in a hurry, but there was too little warning time to tell our fellow students to hide their cigarettes. Instead, the teacher found herself in the middle of cigarette smoke blowing into her face. At that time, such behaviour was not tolerated, even outside the school hours. If the parents of the smoking students hadn't come up with a written statement allowing their children to smoke, expulsion from school would certainly have been the response. This time, the case was settled without any repercussions for the two students. Fooling around while young is more easily understood than carrying these behaviours into adulthood and leaving these kinds of slip-ups behind.

"Swimming lessons were one particular sports subject at school. The Turku Town indoor pool allowed alternate days for public use. On one day, males could use the facility and on the other day, female visitors used it. This reflected the Finnish culture, which allowed for naked swimming. Some young people, like me, nurtured however, some reservations towards naked swimming, particularly with others. To stay away from swimming lessons required a letter from home. The exemption, which was then granted, was offered in exchange for other activities. One of these was making notes of old gravestones in the local cemetery and giving them a visual facelift by clearing away the weeds. This substitute for swimming lessons was not exactly popular, leading often to arrangements between classmates. Taking turns, one student made the gravestone notes while the other went about enjoying freedom away from school duties. In hindsight, we really didn't know whether or not the teachers turned a blind eye on the cemetery visitors as long as 'humbug' didn't come to their attention.

"It was during these swimming lessons that cheeky female classmates would have a go at others about their appearance, often challenging the sensitive self-confidence of young teens. Such behaviour came and went again, at least helping over time to strengthen our resolve. By learning to ignore this kind of unfairness, it prepared us to become stronger later in life. We all have to go through a learning process, no matter how small life's challenges might be. It all helped to build a stronger personality. Thus, *it became the direction which I slowly adopted; not only during swimming lessons, but in the way I approached life in my future years."*

Recently, Finland was recognized internationally as having one of the best performing education systems in the world. Finland still functions today with just the single public education system, which provides equal opportunities for all its citizens.

The fact that 'Mikael Agricola', a contemporary Christian reformer with Martin Luther, unified its relatively small population during the 16th century later played a vital role in support of this education system. Especially in recent history, all community efforts went into one public education system, slowly resulting in the highly recognized standards of today. It is also not by accident that countries with a focus on private education parallel to a public one do not reach the same overall recognition for their education systems. Finland has a long-standing tradition with compulsory school attendance from about 1865.

Arja's grandpa proudly told her of his time at school when schooling hadn't yet reached all the smaller places in the country. He attended school for just two weeks, which in his view was enough to lead his life and satisfy the literacy test of the church before his marriage. From early on, it was compulsory in Finland to read and write out of the Lutheran bible to a level satisfactory to the pastor before a marriage was sanctified.

There are many historical Finnish facts that tell about the birth of this nation. Many people of today's Finland take much of this history for granted, conveniently forgetting that their forefathers made sacrifices so that they could live today a life of natural enjoyment. Aleksi Kivi, a Finnish writer of the 19th century, is recognized as the father of the Finnish language. This is despite Michael Agricola having already established the first 'ABC book' and the translation of the Bible's 'New Testament' into Finnish almost three hundred years earlier.

Kivi describes in his play 'The Seven Brothers', the great epos of the Finnish tribe in which over a 1000 years history can be recognized for every Finn. From the 'Kalevala' and 'Nomad' times, the harsh realities of a battle with nature with wolves, bears, and the climate caused enduring suffering. This led to constantly battling the shortcomings of Finland's farming culture. It continued until the modern époque in which the literacy test became just one small cultural step in the early education efforts of Finland.

Together with Swedish, the Finnish language mainly survived because of the peasants who, during historical times, generally couldn't read. This fact is interesting in as much as it demonstrates that language culture has always derived from somewhere other than 'higher societal ranks'. Probably, the 'Academie Francaise' of France has been the only institutionalised exception to this general trend.

Earlier, the Finnish language was regarded as a lower class language in comparison to Swedish, until it was declared an official language jointly with Swedish in 1883. After the independence declaration of Finland in 1917, one more flare-up occurred during the Civil War between 1917 up to 1919. The Finnish identity was once more brought into question. One political side in Finland wanted to join the 'Bolsheviks' of Russia at that time, calling themselves the 'Reds', while others, the 'Whites', opted for an independent Finland. Interestingly, both sides were standing *for* the Finnish language. Thus it was that, between the two powers, the Finnish language identity decided an outcome for Finland again.

It was the peasants who mainly preserved the Finnish identity. Many could only lease land from higher-ranking citizens, just to be allowed to toil long and hard to make a tough living. This was still happening right up to the beginning of the 20th Century. Here the language also played a major role in Finland's history, surviving with the majority of its people, the 'peasant underdogs'. Once more, it shows that changes have always come from the strong base of societies and not from their so-called 'higher ranks'.

During her school years, Arja went through primary levels in Turku followed by three senior classes in Nokia, near Tampere. School days started at 8 o'clock in the morning, following the timetable into the afternoon with a midday break. At this time, the school canteen served a hot lunch free of charge to all pupils regardless of social class.

Children from the age of seven were under school supervision for most of the day prompting from early on this lunch arrangement, which still operates today. Such regulations helped parents share with the school in the upbringing of a younger generation by giving some time back to the parents during the day. The school week was not five days as it is today, but six days including occasionally a whole Saturday. All school subjects were taught so that at the end of a school career students generally had a broad knowledge basis, which furthered life's journey for each child.

Students rarely complained of being overworked by school subjects in these times. Therefore, the question arises, who made the decision to cut back on time spent at school and the content studied while there? Carried out under the pretext of taking stress out of school for a younger generation, it has resulted today in only more problems maintaining appropriate discipline in school classes.

During the summer months of June, July, and August, holidays released all students from school disciplines. A long winter had ensured everybody had an abundance of explosive longings for outdoor living. Nature awakened during long, sunny, often balmy summer days. Not all years brought a good summer to this far northern part of the globe, but when it happened, compensation with satisfaction is guaranteed for the long winter waiting period.

Most of the average families living in the city had another place of their own, often shared with others, along the coast of the Baltic Sea or inland shores of lakes. There were more than 60 000 of these to spread mainly across the centre and southern part of the country. Even people catching up in summer with outside work, which they couldn't do during winter, were also out for pleasure just like everybody else. They too wanted to spend some time in a timber cottage near the shores of beautiful lakes surrounded by forests.

Swimming, boating, and fishing with line or net were the main activities, along with the obligatory visits to the timber sauna hut. The sauna huts were usually found near the water, which led over a short pier into deeper water. Here, during summer, quickly grown high grass with an abundance of early summer flowers mixed in between the lake's shore, allowing a swim or a boating trip. A life closer to nature is the summer wish of every Finn.

In those years, around the 1950s, time spent outside Finland wasn't commonly affordable. However, shipping between Finland and Sweden, around southwest Finland and through the archipelago of innumerable islands, provided one of the best opportunities for a stay outside the country.

Arja's home in 'Honkaisteranta', outside Turku, was located near the sea, and her family also had another house on the other side of town on the shores of a freshwater 'arm' of the sea. Sure enough, this house in 'Auvaisberri' was the property of father Petteri, but the family still shared a stay in it especially in later years. The biggest choice was whether to seek time off near seawater or freshwater.

Summer holidays were in those days so significant in a young life that many often remember this time into their adult life. During summer time in Finland, people needed a night's rest too, even when the sun looked through house windows for most of the night hours. Shutters, curtains or both immersed the inside of the house into dimmed twilight. The sinking sun reached the horizon about 11 pm, resting only for three hours and sending from the horizon, dark red light beams into the sky.

Arja remembers getting out of bed around 6 o'clock in the morning. "Life outside was already in full swing during the first four sunny hours of the day. ' Slippy', our terrier, already waited behind the door of my room, jumping straight into my bed and waiting for me to return a few minutes later after I had pushed the curtains aside to allow a flood of sunlight to enter my room.

"Mum had started the day in the kitchen and was already waiting for me to join in the breakfast preparation. On one of those days off school, I decided to stay

a bit longer in bed, because there was no need to get ready for school. I grabbed my adventure book and started reading in the company of 'Slippy' until Mum turned up; reminding me that some work needed to be done inside and outside the house, before planning for the rest of the day.

"My sister wasn't up yet, waiting for a special invitation. Usually when I had finished in the bathroom, turning up dressed in the kitchen, Mum then went over to my sister's room, shaking her out of bed. Mum herself had next to no sleep during the night as father Petteri didn't turn up at home again as usual, busy with his own way of a life."

In those days, the breakfast table held brown, ring rye bread, crisp bread, butter, cooked porridge, and a glass of fresh milk supplied to the doorstep by the milkman on weekdays. Blueberry or cranberry jam, pickled herring with onions or cucumber, block cheese, and local apples in late summer were also found on the table. An orange or banana was a rare sight in those days; many people haven't ever seen them.

As Petteri saw himself ahead of his time, he indeed managed occasionally to turn up with those tropical fruits of which nobody really knew the origin at that time. During breakfast, Arja's mother also mentioned briefly the day's program, especially during summer holidays. After the allocated work for the day was completed, the promise was made of some time away from home at their other place in 'Auvaisberri' while Tysse would arrange simultaneously some business in town.

These were special times for Arja. "For me, this meant I could see my best friend Tuija, who lived by then in a town flat. What an incentive to get my day's chores finished quickly! Tidying up my bedroom, a little help in the kitchen, feeding the dog, spending a few moments in the garden paying special attention to my own veggie patch – all were completed promptly. Meanwhile, children from the neighbourhood already waited at the front gate to the road for my sister to join them. On some days, I also took part in a ball game on the road in front of the house or went for a swim on the shore at the lower end of our garden. Mum reminded me constantly not to forget the time. However, as soon as time allowed, I took refuge again with my books."

The morning hours passed unnoticed and it was only hunger that told the children that time had rushed close to midday. Tysse was getting ready for town, the wash only waited to be hung up on the washing line in the garden. The bus to town passed twice a day so one had to make sure not to miss it. Other people from the area were also on the bus and usually started some brief conversation about their families. People knew each other well as most called the area home for a good number of years.

Before heading for the bus stop, which was only a short distance away from home, Tysse had prepared a basket of food to take to the 'Auvaisberri' summerhouse. People usually got off the bus in the city-square centre where, on Wednesday, the market was a colourful display of benches with flowers, veggies and fruit of the current season. Tent booths offered fresh fish while others had meat; all was stored away in iceboxes, as fridges were not so common yet, which meant that everything had to be consumed very quickly.

Another trip into the nearby shopping centre ensured the most needed items for home were purchased. While Tysse looked after most of the shopping in the company of Raija - Arja's mother and sister loved shopping more than she did - Arja went to visit her friend Tuija at a nearby address. At Tuija's place, conversation had to be kept short so as not to miss the bus departure. Before leaving for the bus, Tuija's mum usually offered a little refreshment, which supplied much needed energy for the rest of the day. Breakfast was almost half a day behind. After disembarking from the bus, it was only a short walking distance through the forest to our summerhouse. The day had advanced into the afternoon hours but because it was summer, a good number of daylight hours still remained.

On arrival, the house was unlocked from the veranda side. The house itself rested on timber all laid upon a granite step, which climbed up the short distance to the house. It was not far from the water's shore. Everything inside the house was orderly right through to the second storey just, as we had previously left it. The house could just as well have been left unlocked, because at that time nobody would even have thought of stealing anything from other people.

Neighbours from further out of the city usually knew each other and had a good understanding with each other. Generally speaking, Finns are not the best conversationalists. They would rather keep to themselves, but they are friendly nevertheless. Petteri had demonstrated to his family that alcohol frees the tongue of many Finns. Rather than a positive thing, this can be seen as a national plague. Distribution of alcohol in those days was still strictly controlled until 1969 when officials acted. Rather than restricting the supply of alcohol, officials took the step of regulating its consumption by increasing the price accordingly. An initial rush on alcohol triggered through this liberalisation soon settled down into a more reasonable consumer demand. Arja's mother made sure alcohol was not brought to the summerhouse, but Petteri still managed to have his drinks.

Tysse made sure that her children kept away from any alcohol because it is a daunting life experience to see what alcohol does to families and their budgets. She kept a close eye on the family budget, never allowing the essentials for the family to run out. This meant that a constant battle raged against Petteri's generosity and the family's needs. Tysse usually won.

One of the first chores in the summerhouse was to get the sauna started in the small timber hut on the edge of the shore. While her mum re-arranged the inside of the house, Arja chopped the wood for the sauna.

"Next to one side of the house lay a pile of wooden blocks cut on a horseshoe in regular lengths waiting to be split with an axe on a leftover tree post. This time it was my turn to tackle the job. I carefully watched each block of wood steadily positioned on top of the post so I could hit the block's centre gently with the knife-edge of the axe. If the split pieces didn't fall straight to the side, I was told not to try again, because it was too dangerous. The axe had then to be reversed together with the wood block

wedged on it and swung with the back of the axe on to the block. The block was too heavy for me to lift at this stage.

"My little sister liked to watch me while constantly passing comments. I tried my best to ignore her and not get angry, saying to myself, "You are the little one and deserve to only watch me." Chopped up wood pieces were placed in a bound basket to be carried down to the sauna oven."

A timber door with a glass window gave access to the sauna, a small room in which all the walls were neatly panelled in northern aspen wood. The offset position of the door ensured the two wooden slat-platforms could go along the whole opposite length of the room in front of the oven, which was located in the centre. A solid cast iron oven-base, slightly raised from the timber floor on four legs, opened via a heavy swing door. The usual newspaper and twigs helped get a fire started. The split wood pieces followed immediately to maintain the fire.

The other wood in the basket was stored outside in a stack under the protection of the roof extension. Both the sauna and oven door remained shut until the embers shrank sufficiently to give room for more wood in order to maintain a good heat. On top of the oven, there were basalt rock pieces, securely enclosed to absorb some of the rising heat. This heat also radiated from the shiny stovepipe leading through the timber ceiling to the chimney, which stuck out of the roof in square set bricks.

A shiny metal ladle in a pot of water was on the floor next to the lower bench. This ladle was used to pour water over the heated rocks when the sauna room reached an optimum temperature - about 80 degrees Celsius. A wall spiral-thermometer showed the temperature. The vapour from the stones then rises up, instantly heating the air with moisture. A prickling of the skin indicates the rising temperature, which reaches its zenith in the highest area of the sauna under the ceiling. Exposing the head to this peak temperature can be uncomfortable, but there is always the option of stepping down one level or lying down on one of the stepped wooden slat-platforms.

Everything in the sauna is indicative of the high temperature except timber, which is why a sauna is built completely out of timber. Even the handle of the door and the water ladle is fitted with timber because metal would cause severe burns on contact. A timber rail the shape of the oven protects it. Sauna visitors know to keep the door shut tightly to maintain the sauna heat.

As the body exudes more the longer and higher up one sits in the sauna, it is the general practice to place a towel on the timber bench before sitting down so that the smooth untreated timber surfaces remain hygienic. Temperature and time in a sauna is governed by individual preferences. There are plenty of variables to make the sauna enjoyable: sitting or lying on a lower or higher bench and how often water is sprinkled over the hot rocks. In addition, a light beating with fresh, leafy, birch tree twigs over the back, legs, and arms assists visibly with blood circulation, giving the skin a reddish tinge. At the same time, a beautiful perfume from the birch leaves fills the hot sauna air.

An hourglass mounted in an easily visible position on the timber wall assists with keeping an eye on the time in a sauna. Too long in a sauna is not recommended. It is better to have more short visits in succession. Some people begin and end their sauna experience by washing in cold water out of a bucket. Others, whose houses have water right at the doorstep, like Arja's, take a swim straight out of the sauna.

After a sauna, a healthy body should feel like a newborn baby as hardly anyone can become cleaner than through sauna. It is also a traditional focus for the Finns; sauna gives warmth, cleanliness, hygiene, relaxation, and a meeting place (everybody has the same equalising naked status). All of this has helped shape Finnish culture over a long period of history. In addition, Finns have a migration history, which included the essential cultural element of sauna, remaining to modern times a firm part of the Finnish everyday life. Sauna visits take place at any time during the whole year. Not even the cold winter snow or ice, stop Finns pursuing their sauna. In summer, there is cold water in the bucket and in winter, the snow or hole in the ice of a frozen lake has the same effect.

The change from sweating in the sauna to rolling in the snow or swimming in an ice hole is so extreme that it is obvious participants are in very good health. This heat absorption in a sauna and cold shock therapy to follow greatly stabilises the body's thermo-regulation. Sauna not only cleans externally, but also internally as long as it is not overdone. Life is like this: In everything we do, only the right balance can deliver the 'goods'.

Ice hole visits in winter can also turn into a more dangerous, rather than a refreshing exercise, as Arja experienced while skating with her sister on the frozen surface near their home shore area. In the dim sunlight during the day, a layer of freshly fallen snow transformed the whole area into uniformly white winter scenery in which only the forest indicated where the land rose out of the sea. For weeks, the winter cold had increased the ice thickness, not only of the lakes, but also of the seawater. The fact that salty seawater had frozen completely across the sea arm bordering the property, was a strong indication of how cold temperatures had become. Even during the day, it was just in excess of minus 25 degree Celsius.

"On that day, my sister and I were not ice skating on our own. From the opposite shore, people came on the ice too. From a distance, nobody could tell whether the skaters were children or adults out looking for enjoyment. On such an icy cold winter's day, everybody was packed into thick clothes, which didn't even reveal whether it was a male or female beneath the layers. Like most of the others, we've also learned by previous experience, to enjoy ice-skating by not having too many close encounters with the hard ice. Over time, everybody avoids the sinking feeling when the feet run away too quickly, sending us with our heaviest part first on to the ice. Alas, each time, it does hurt!

"This time however, we hit a snag in a spot right in the centre of the frozen sea arm and rather closer to the shore, where one expected it the least. A snowfield covered a weak ice spot, sending my sister falling into the icy water. Quick action became the priority, as did pursuing the right action in such a situation. For me, the right thing was lying down flat on the ice surface near the hole and extending my hastily removed winter jacket in its full length, to my sister in the ice hole. Screaming like a banshee, she struggled to stay afloat near the surface, every so often disappearing beneath it.

"Trying to get a hold on the ice edge would have been a futile exercise for my sister. Every second counted as her heavy winter clothes became drenched with water making her dangerously heavier by the minute. I was in shock myself, but also knew not to waste one moment. The two arms of my jacket fortunately proved strong enough for both of us to get hold of an end each. I was then able to slowly, but surely pull Raija head first out of the water onto the ice. To help me move backwards I had to remain flat on the ice and dig the points of my shoes into the ice surface to prevent me from sliding towards the ice hole. I remained aware and cautious enough not to weaken the ice either by vibrations of my body or my foothold.

"Urgent but steady, secure action was needed to get my sister out of the icy water quickly. Usually only a few valuable moments are granted in such a rescue mission. "You are not a light sister," was all I could say. Standard recommendations of putting a bar, a plank or even a ski across the ice hole was not an option, because none of these was on hand or close enough to help. Time would not have allowed the luxury of searching for these things.

"It was equally important that I didn't risk myself sliding into this ice hole. This happens every winter when people take too high a risk in a rescue or try to help in the wrong way, ending up risking their own lives. Unfortunately, it does sometimes happen that the rescuer ends up in the ice hole, turning the whole event into a less successful effort. Usually, one of the two prevents the other staying afloat long enough to survive.

"I knew from my parents not to walk near the broken ice surface in order to try to give a hand to the person in the ice hole. This would almost certainly cause the rescuer to also fall into the ice hole. Once my sister was out of the hole and lying flat on the ice - after exhausting efforts from both of us - I continued to lie flat on the ice when moving towards Raija. In order to help her, I knew she urgently needed to get rid of her heavily soaked, padded jacket. This would reduce the crucial weight before she could start to move on her own, across the few metres of ice around the hole until a stronger ice layer further apart could support her sufficiently to get up on her feet.

"No time was left to waste even after the rescue was completed. We both needed to head straight home to get our wet clothes off, especially my sister, who needed to seek bed warmth and then a sauna. Sauna can give a helping hand in more than just relaxation cases. At the time, nobody else was at home, giving us time to get over the worst before mum arrived. In hindsight, it was also easier then to explain what happened."

It is necessary to follow some important rules on the regular visits to an ice hole for a swim after a sauna. Firstly, a timber ladder should lead into the ice hole from the fixed point of a boat landing bridge. This is necessary because it would virtually be impossible to pull yourself onto the ice edge and out onto the surface of the ice. Moreover, the ladder needs to be timber, quite simply because a metal one could cause the body to be stuck on the metal in the extremely cold weather conditions. This could easily lead to the skin becoming separated when forced off carelessly. Perhaps the most important part of this message was never ever to touch metal with the tongue, because it will inevitably be stuck, frozen to the metal in a most inconvenient, painful way.

Winter walk – Finland

The extreme cold conditions during most winters in the far north of Europe impose special rules on everyone. For instance, when outside, especially under windy conditions, it is very important to be watching one's companions for early signs of frostbite. These usually appear first on the exposed face and then on hands and feet. Skin turning from a natural pink into a bluish colour in different spots, are the first harbingers of frostbite. What would appear to be the sensible first measure in seeking warmth is, unfortunately, the wrong approach. The affected area is cooled under the skin even more than just on the surface. The frostbite indicates that the body needs to take the inside energy to the surface to fight the frostbite symptoms. Warming up from the outside still wouldn't reach the deeper areas, eventually leaving, in due time, the damage to progress. The only effective measure is rubbing the frostbite area with snow so that the circulation from inside gradually is supplying the warmth that went missing during an idle exposure to the cold. Discoloured white skin spots appearing in the cold are alarming signs that the area is on the verge of dying from the cold. This is often painful, after effect can be lessened best by the cold massage with snow.

One false belief is that alcohol seems to be one of the measures to beat the cold. However, this can only have an inverse effect by either causing the person to become insensitive to the cold or by stressing the body thereby failing to allow the re-energisation of vital body functions. This might sound trivial to someone who is not aware of the problems that alcohol has caused in Finland within its population. The fallout of it is a concern for many. Arja was lucky that her dad, Petteri, could consume whatever he wanted without showing a sign of intoxication. He learned his lesson later when he passed away with severe stomach cancer at much too early an age. With winter left behind, it was time to return to the summerhouse in Auvaisberri, where soon after arriving the sauna had been started. In summer, the swim between sauna visits was much less demanding than that of wintertime. While enjoying this recreation, Arja remembers her Mum calling from the house veranda, higher up the rocky slope, "If you want something for dinner, you'd better go out with the boat and catch some fish."

The day meanwhile had progressed into the afternoon, leaving the summer sun still high up in the sky, which provided more than enough time to take out the boat for fishing. The family kept a small rowing boat in Auvaisberri, anchored between the many rocks that lined the shore near the sauna hut. Here and there, a little sandy spot appeared, not going far into the water. The shore dropped almost immediately, without transition, steeply into the dark, calm water. Arja's friend, Tuija, joined her in picking up the pair of oars, a simple fishing rod and the bucket for the fish. They also needed a knife to prepare the fish straight after a catch. Before freeing the boat, they made sure they loaded up a bottle of homemade ginger drink, because after a sauna, a drink is a welcome necessity. After Tuija and Arja had scooped out the water in the boat with a bucket, one of them took the seat on the board that went across the centre, engaging first one oar into a fork then followed by the second one on the opposite boat rim. The oar on the shore side gently pushed the boat away, leaving the other girl to jump quickly into the boat so as not to be left behind. Meanwhile Arja's little sister helped her mother with work in the kitchen and the house – mainly cooking the young potatoes until the duo returned with their catch.

The memories of these fishing trips on languid summer days remained with Arja. "Further out on the lake, fish were snapping at insects near the water's surface, an indication that the time for fishing was right. What kind of fish would bite our fishing rod was due mainly to luck. In the case of something bigger hooking onto our rod, a catching net on a wooden stick also went on board with us. As bait, we used anything that fish could possibly eat, ranging from breadcrumbs to chunks of cheese, from life bugs to worms, dug out and collected in the few spots near the shoreline. Curious little sardines were the first things we hooked and caught out of the water in the net. Shortly after, we were lucky enough to catch a perch or a haddock.

"The air hovered still and warm over the water from these long, sunny, summer days. Insects sought a refreshing drink while fish came up to snatch them, a perfect natural cycle in which we've entered, catching the fish. Out of the air, swallows occasionally cruised in a zigzag pattern just above the water; taking their share of insects while indicating at the same time that rain was not far away. These conditions favoured the catch of the day. We didn't have to wait long for a good-sized fish to pull on the line, trying to get its share out of this feeding frenzy. Two or three good-sized perches plus the little sardines was plenty for dinner. The fish were cut open from underneath and cleaned out. They then went into the bin filled with water in our boat.

"Time allowed us also to watch the bird life from surrounding forests as they measured their territories. From the smaller to the larger, ouzel, sparrows, and a group of wild brown-green feathered ducks; all were seen at various times. There was even the occasional white goose that, with a heavy wing stroke, took off from the water into the air. On previous boating trips in the area, with even more time up our sleeves, we patiently rested with the boat in one or another spot to watch a buzzard in a forest clearing next to the lake's water. It was diving for something on the ground and lifting it in a rush high up into a tree with its large wingspan batting the air for height."

If luck was on the side of the girls, they might see a beaver carrying branches across land to its burrow, a very rare encounter in Finland's harsh environment. Over a short period, summer returns a plentiful supply of those things that have been scarce during the harsh winter months. Survival is a difficult and complex issue for most of the year during a long winter. The attentive eye can then watch the grazing elk beside the common magpie, crow or raven and sometimes even a white swan peacefully floating in the water. Observing nature can teach many lessons, which embrace a lifetime. Everything in nature reflects a beauty from birth up until death, as long as peace dominates.

As the sun sinks later in the day, mosquitoes come out of hiding in millions. It was important that the two little 'fisher-girls' made sure to be back with their catch of fish before the mosquitoes descended. During summer, Finland's mosquitoes can be a daunting plague. Not all years are the same however; some years they are missing completely. In the north of Lapland especially, mosquitoes grow during the long summer months to sizes seen nowhere else in the world and consequently can make life very difficult. Fortunately, in the south of the country where Arja grew up, they were usually of a much smaller size. Her father once commented about his experience with mosquitoes in Lapland during the war, "They were our greatest enemies."

In the summerhouse, as the day progressed towards the evening, hunger reminded the whole family that it was time for dinner. The big, long table on the veranda could seat many more than the family of four. The remaining space could be filled with a monopoly game and sometimes during the year, mostly before Christmas, even the oval track of a small, metal model railway. The train set found room in the midst of other items like books and a tray showing shiny, reddish apple faces.

Father Petteri always had something from Sweden organised for Arja and Raija. However, the things he brought home first became his toys and only after his interest and excitement waned, did the girls get the go-ahead to look after them. As well as the model railway, there was a racecourse with model racing cars, all operated at that time by hand. From time to time, Petteri spent up big, bringing into the home all sorts of stuff, which was mainly for his pleasure.

However, there were also times that he was short of money and everybody knew it. This is when Petteri became tacit. In such an event, Arja's mum had, quite regularly, a struggle finding the money to pay the bills. Luckily, Petteri stowed away his money in a disorderly fashion, using whatever place could be found. He easily lost track of these places, giving Tysse a chance to find it. For instance, she regularly 'struck gold' in a pocket of his clothes before they ended up in a tub for washing.

A life-sized doll from England regularly took a seat at the table next to Arja. It was a doll that followed her throughout her entire life. The doll's name, 'Princess Elizabeth', was a reference to the throne successor in England, who became Queen in 1952. A bunch of freshly cut flowers, collected each day out of the garden also had a regular place on the table too. Before dinner, Tysse always lit a set of candles in a branched stand so that all the family could see the invitation to gather at the table, bestowing on a late afternoon a touch of festivity. Dinner was not only to share food, but it was also the time devoted to a family meeting.

It was still a number of years before television was introduced. In the meantime, radio informed everybody around the dinner table of current events and entertained with music. From the seat along one side of the table, there were views through the veranda's glass windows out over the lake's water. Tongues of forested land have taken over in the distance and the forest shade around the house still hadn't reached the calm, dark water further down along the shore.

As soon as dinner was over, some time of the day was left for playing outside the house. Arja and her sister took turns at doing the dishes, which were done in a bowl on an appointed small timber table on the side of the house. Dishes were left in a wooden X-stand on the table to dry off on its own in usually less than half an hour. Water had to be carried in a bucket from the lake or an underground well further inland and away from the house. Water needed for washing came from the lake while drinking water was taken from the well. There was no running water in the summerhouse at this time.

After the kitchen work was finished, badminton helped pass some time. The table was set up on the limited flat land under the veranda. When the weather didn't allow outside play, there was always inside where, above the second floor, there was a billiard table and round darts board with its marked rings and numbers.

Apart from the approaching weekend, the family planned a number of holidays in the summer residence at Auvaisberri. Most of these days were filled with swimming, sauna, boating, visiting neighbours, and outdoor and indoor recreational activities. There was never time for boredom. When Petteri happened to turn up, he would have brought something amusing along, distracting attention away from questions like, "Where have you been for the last couple of days?" He incorporated the magician and clown all together in one person, never failing to bring the fun with him.

"Those were the memories he mainly bestowed on us," Arja recalls. "My sister, my friend Tuija, kids out of the neighbourhood, including myself, called him 'villi-pappa' (wild dad). Only mum could see behind this 'circus', telling us that dad always knew to make a show around everything, thus diverting attention from other issues in his life. In fact, it was he claiming to be ahead of his time. Not only did he organise the latest 'swell', trying to set up in town the first illegal red-light district. Despite his talent to engage others in his enterprises, this particular one failed. Moreover, another shoddy enterprise was the illegal drug trafficking, which came to the attention of the local police. They caught everybody else except Petteri, including, on one occasion, people we called friends."

During her childhood, Arja wasn't aware of all this of course. Together with her few friends and the rest of the family, she rather enjoyed his fantasy expressions with their positive aspects and so Petteri remained in the memories of many of the children. The other sides of his life were the shadows of his bright side: the one who shines, inevitably lives also in his own shadow. Petteri's strong personality won him people's respect in the first place, while only insiders could really know better that there was more behind the shiny façade than the eye could see. But again, 'What the eye doesn't see, the heart doesn't grieve over'.

"Such a reality mainly accounted for my sister and me, but over time mum couldn't see the brighter sides any longer. Keeping everything doubtful away from us,

my mother secured for me the happy years of my childhood. However, this didn't stop depriving her of much needed sleep at night, while she waited in vain too many times for dad to stay at home with his family."

As time progressed, Petteri bought a sandpit on the outskirts of the city of Turku from a Swedish-speaking gentleman. The pit was directly alongside an inland lake. During the summer months Arja's father now spent most of his time organising the sand and loading it onto his trucks. A modest timber hut with only one side window and a centrally located door gave shelter on site. This soon attracted the local kids' attention after they heard that the previous owner has been a retired sea captain. Word had it that he occasionally turned up on a visit with a huge, bright green parrot, which he had brought from South America.

Arja particularly wanted to see that parrot and couldn't wait for the sea captain to visit the sand pit. She and Raija began to spend time in the hut on the summer weekends, actually enjoying the much smaller space compared with that of the family's home or summerhouse. Its size and little outfit induced children to live easily in a fairytale home of 'Little Snow White'. The girls happily played out their own scenes. Arja and Raija had a very happy, unburdened childhood with hardly any problems. This was mainly down to their mother who always leaned towards the simple life in which money wasn't an obvious issue. Instead, the children learned to entertain themselves while keeping a distance from life's inevitable mixture of experiences. Many of these experiences could be better tackled from the distance of adulthood.

When the seaman arrived in an old, paint-faded passenger car, the parrot sat on the front seat next to him. This made an extraordinary impression because nobody had seen this type of thing in Finland before. The elderly man had a thick dark beard around his whole face, which made him look as if he had just arrived from a far away continent like South America on a long, long journey. Petteri walked over from the sandpit near the lake to assist our guests in getting out of the car. The gentleman spoke mainly Swedish despite his living in Finland. This however, wasn't something totally outside our experience as officially, Swedish was also accepted in Finland. Over past centuries, the close political connections of the two countries had led to an affiliation. The Swedish taught at school wasn't exactly up to scratch with the younger generation, but the older generation could converse better at that time.

Regardless of this fact, Arja, her sister Raija, her friend Tuija, and another school friend from the neighbourhood, singularly focussed their attention on the parrot. The bird remained motionless on the other front seat even after the characteristically nautical seaman came to stand with rather shaky legs outside the car. It was as if he had been on a long sea voyage. Johansson, the seaman, went straight across to the other side of the car and opened the front door calling the parrot by its name, 'Laura'. Prior to this, he pushed his left arm into a leather sleeve that sat on the seat behind Laura.

Johansson was totally fascinating when he started to sing a Finnish nursery rhyme with his grumpy voice. When he stopped, the bird repeated the melody incredibly accurately and only then moved with its strong claws onto the outstretched left arm of Johansson, who meanwhile had moved his hand right in front of Laura. Together they emerged from the car. Both of Laura's claws were firmly around the leather-protected arm and ensured it stood level with the top of Johansson's head. What a beautiful, majestic creature this was. Laura moved its head slowly sideways after confirming, with piercing eye contact with everybody who stood around, that everything was to its liking.

As Arja, driven by curiosity, moved closer to Laura, she remembers her fear. "I became frightened by its sudden response, "Get out!" The bird's voice was so sonorously commanding that only by repeating the song of Johansson could Laura be settled down again. Music apparently must have been its favourite method of communication. It certainly didn't attempt to move from its steady, upright position on the leather sleeve. Then I cautiously attempted singing a couple of notes that I knew of the rhyme. Laura instantly turned towards me, not only repeating the whole melody again but also attempting to move over to me.

"My first reaction to this was that I stepped backwards rather quickly as I wasn't convinced about taking Laura onto my arm. Looking at the three large articulated claws on each of the two feet, I knew they wouldn't do my unprotected arm any good. Johansson however encouraged me to bring my arm into line with his so that he could push the leather sleeve together with Laura on to my arm. Said and done, Laura then looked curiously into my eyes. Fascinated to the point of forgetting about fear, I started to talk Finnish words to my new friend. All Laura wanted however was for me to continue with the melody.

"As I couldn't immediately respond because of my limited musical talent, the bird moved from one leg onto the other, probably indicating that it wanted to return to its master. My talk obviously didn't please Laura, so to stop its claws from digging anymore firmly into my arm; I once more began to sing. My efforts to repeat notes out of the song turned the parrot calm again, happy enough to join in after I had finished. Laura turned out to be the better musician and it appeared that it wanted me to learn better from its song. However, Laura was becoming heavier on my arm by the minute so that I had to use my other arm to support it from underneath. Laura was not accepting this. Its melody instantly stopped, changing into a deep hoarse voice emerging from the strong, downwards-crooked beak."

The moment then had arrived when Laura moved back over to its owner in the same way it had come on to Arja's arm. Peace had from then on returned, no talking, no singing any more, the parrot must have said enough to its liking. It made not one visible attempt to use its big wings, which entirely covered the bright, shiny green plumage covering the body. Laura must have forgotten how to fly. Were climate and the natural environment too different here from where it came from?

Anyhow, Arja enjoyed this encounter tremendously; because it was unlikely she would ever again experience such a magnificent creature from such a close distance. The whole appearance of this bird-of-paradise had something of its own in its resting elegance. Everybody must have given Laura an impression of curiosity, judging from its steady position, first on the car seat and then outside on the arm. According to the seaman, Laura was very old, even measured in terms of human years, older than most could live. In fact, it was said the bird was well over one hundred years.

Only when Laura had again taken the front seat inside the car, was the door closed again. Everybody else had moved away leaving the seaman, the parrot and Arja alone with the farewell. Both Johansson and Laura had given themselves a break during their day in an excursion out of the city to visit the sandpit. The others must have felt insecure to come face to face with such characters as the seaman and his parrot, while this extraordinary meeting just served to fascinate Arja. As they had come by car, so the couple left again for the more familiar home in town.

Much later, when Arja and her own family lived in Brazil in a natural parrot habitat, she couldn't get that close to such a magnificent creature. Not even in Brazil could she see its best-known relation, the colourful giant parrot, the macaw, which is the bird closest in size to Laura. It was only in the non-natural habitat of Hawaii where Arja later visited with her husband, that they came to see two macaws in a totally enclosed aviary.

WhileLauralivedawell-protectedlifeunderthe care of the seaman (even sheltered from the severe Finnish winters), an estimated larger number of those parrot-giants live today in captivity all over the world. There are many more than nature can hold in its few shrinking natural habitats. When will we lose the last 'Laura' in nature's paradise? Hardly any other creature had made such a lasting impression on Arja as this parrot encountered in her homeland of Finland. It is only people who have experienced such an unexpected encounter with one of nature's impressive creatures behaving so human-like, probably would fully comprehend just how touched she was.

The day in the sandpit 'resort' had welcomed a change to the otherwise more customary holiday activities of swimming, boating, sauna, playing a few games and collecting berries. In the nearby forests, blueberries ripened in the middle of summer and cranberries at the end. Berry picking has always been a quiet, forest business, away from the city noise.

It is not only humans who seek the silence of the Finnish forests; mister 'bruin' also likes collecting his share of summer berries. Occasionally there is a meeting with people unexpectedly seeking the same dainty morsels. In the south where Arja's family lived, bear encounters were mostly unheard of but not in the eastern parts of Karelija towards the Russian border. This area had been part of Finland before World War II, confiscated by Russia in the general confusion of post-war times.

The girls were often told that, while picking berries in the forest, it is good practice to constantly talk to somebody or sing a song. This helps not only to fill in the time but also to let mister 'bruin' know that somebody else is collecting in the forest too. An otherwise sudden meeting with a bear can unleash its territorial defence instincts and it is highly unlikely that the human counterpart could hold his/her territory.

Although there was always the distant likelihood of coming face to face with a bear while searching through the forest for a good share of berries, the girls usually kept talking to each other anyway and didn't mind changing the song occasionally. Some years, berries were in abundance and so large that the baskets filled in a very short time, leaving enough time for tasting the berries along the way. Picking berries at that time was enjoyable and not so much regarded as work, which was reflected in the baskets' contents. Not every time were they filled and when it could be achieved, not everybody reached this goal. It really didn't matter, as all the baskets were stored with their collection in a bigger box at home. Because of picking the berries, hands and mouths were always unmistakably tinged, mainly from the blueberries. On arriving home, only the sauna could deliver an adequate cleaning solution to such an obstinate stain.

The reward for time spent in picking berries from the forest was a treat not only of fresh berries. Waiting in the kitchen was a little pastry to be filled with berries as well as homemade ice cream. Summer holidays were the time for berries. Strawberries at that time were not so common, depending on the summer; they mainly came from nurseries. The wild strawberries from the forest however, were scarce, but tasted much spicier despite their smaller size compared to that of farmed ones. In addition, raspberries could be found on bushes in a few isolated spots. One of the favourite types of berry was the cranberry, which collected during the late summer, produced a diverse taste between sweet, sour, and slightly bitter. They were also very juicy when pressed raw into a jam, going excellently with a dinner including meats.

In the home garden outside the city, gooseberry and redcurrant bushes supplied only a small crop, but brought a welcome variety to the daily menu. Apples, on the other hand, grew only into small sizes on well-protected trees. This was the main fruit availability in Arja's youth. In terms of what is readily available today, it was minimal variety and fruit like oranges and bananas were still unknown in the area. However, what wasn't known about at the time wasn't really missed. Life during childhood followed its course and there was no feeling of inferiority about not having all the choices available now in the new Millennium. Arja grew up naturally happy with only a few food options.

The only other holiday attraction during summer for Arja was a regular visit to her grandparents and aunt in Tampere, Middle Finland. Her mother usually accompanied her on the train, leaving her on arrival in the care of her grandparents because she got along with them quite well. On the other hand, a change from daily life at home could only leave behind the problems standing between her mother and father. In addition, Arja's mum Tysse enjoyed a day or so catching up on the good times in her parents' home before returning alone to Turku.

Arja's sister was not so keen on visiting the grandparents. Raija developed her own way of life much earlier than Arja. It already appeared at an early age that she was more sympathetic towards her dad, whereas Arja sided with mother Tysse. Nevertheless, life with the grandparents during Arja's stay went peacefully by every day. Despite their shop keeping business, they always had time for her. When they were both busy, the aunt who also lived in the house with them, stepped in, listening and eventually answering all the questions children bring up. This early supportive relationship to the family branch in Middle Finland triggered the decision in Arja's later school days to move to Tampere and attend school in Nokia.

An event in 1952, the Olympic Games in Helsinki, put Finland on the world map. Sporting heroes like Paavo Nurmi helped upcoming generations to improve the esteem of sports in Finland. He won nine gold medals and established seventeen world records in the distances between 1,500 and 20,000 metres.

Probably like the majority of Finns, Arja was interested in sport, but not to the extent of competing at a high level. A less energetic pursuit of swimming, outdoors activities and skiing in winter satisfied needs to stay healthy through sports. On a side note, probably not the healthiest one, Coca Cola, the emerging American contribution to the century, used the Olympic Games of Helsinki for the first time as a platform to spread its name. Since then Coca-Cola has become the symbol for American spirit of enterprise, engaging 'goodies' and 'baddies' in a competition.

One of the highlights during the stay in Tampere was a visit to the cinema and open-air theatre in Pynikke to which her aunt usually took Arja. During shows, the film sometimes would stop all of a sudden, needing some time to be restarted. During this time, the theatre was plunged into darkness. After these stoppages, it didn't seem to matter as much when a synchronisation of voices and images did not quite happen. The enjoyment of rare film shows in those days could not be disrupted by technical difficulties. An atmosphere of curiosity mixed with some anxiety remained among the visitors.

From the late 1950s onwards, the introduction of television sets into homes diverted attention away from cinema shows. Petteri naturally was one of the first owners of a television set, bringing it proudly into the family home. Finding time to watch television programs was not so much an issue in the early years after its introduction, because only a couple of hours daily were screened initially, solely in black and white.

Before that time, everybody knew how to pass the time with something useful. Certainly, Arja never experienced boredom. Instead of television, her books kept her entertained. There were more than enough in her grandparents' home. In the course of changes from the home in Turku, Arja experienced differences in Middle Finland at her grandparents' home. The bookshelves in the living room had their own protocol.

"If I wanted a book, I had to ask for it; thus were the rules in the grandparents' home. Moreover, they were the only ones allowed to return it to its original place. Order and cleanliness also contributed to the peaceful atmosphere. There were never arguments, because everybody in the house knew the grandparents' likings and in return, they could respond constantly in a friendly way.

"One thing grand mum couldn't tolerate, was alcohol in the house. Grandpa on the other hand couldn't renounce alcohol completely. Therefore, the compromise was hiding a bottle of schnapps in the 'secret' place behind the wood stack in the cellar. I found out about his secret stash very early on in my stay but I kept his secret safe. That is until one-day grandpa refused to give my visiting cousins and me permission to go outside. It was then that I reminded him of his hidden bottle about which grand mum knew nothing. The trick worked; we went out and grandpa got to keep his secret. What none of us knew however was that grandma skilfully turned a blind eye, pretending to know nothing. It was only many years later that she disclosed to me, "I kept only one eye on the bottle while the other eye looked away; as long as the schnapps didn't leave the house".

"Like me, my aunt spent much of her time reading books while everybody else, like mum and dad at home in Turku, were often too busy during the day to find time to read. A stay with the grandparents always helped cut short school holidays, so when school started again, especially after the three month summer break, school days had already become a distant memory for me."

Teachers, however, made sure to acquaint everybody with school lessons again, sooner rather than later. Back at school, summer gradually changed into autumn with the daylight hours becoming shorter again and nature preparing for the long winter. Memories of summer holidays retreated too, easing the change back to school.

Even by late October, a persistent 'Indian Summer' had given way to a short autumn. Leaves on birch, maple, aspen, oak and willow trees quickly changed into a colourful spectacle before giving way to winter's mighty regime. In the north of Finland, in Lapland, 'ruska' (autumn leaf drop) is seen. Leaves exhibit the colourful autumn palette, indicating that autumn can sometimes happen in as short a time as just one day. These changes can happen virtually overnight, therefore becoming as intense as the opposite part of the year, when winter turns to springtime. Towards winter, life became more and more restricted to indoor living. Sauna and skiing, skating or tobogganing remained the outdoor activities while many other preoccupations 'hibernated' over winter until springtime introduced a short but powerful summer again.

The older houses were built exclusively of timber, supplying effective insulation against the winter's cold. They were commonly painted in a rusty reddish tone, except for door and window frames, which were highlighted in a bright colour, usually white. Today, building materials have considerably changed in Finland, as in the rest of the world, as new insulation materials found application in concrete element buildings.

The nearest school at Turku was built of timber back in 1882 and painted in a different colour, yellow, from residential buildings. As soon as winter introduced the colder temperatures, the school had to be heated to allow lessons to take place. During Arja's early years at school, there was a plan in place to accommodate this. Taking turns, a few students arrived earlier at school to help the keeper in firing up the ovens in each classroom. At first, previously cut timber was used, followed by briquettes so that when the school officially opened at eight o'clock in the morning, everybody could enter into a comfortably heated classroom.

When the outside temperature dropped below minus 25 degree Celsius during the day, school children were not obliged to go to school and the schools remained closed. During the 1950s, going to school on skis was still quite common. In later years, central heating and improved public transport eliminated the absolute dependence of school attendance on weather conditions.

Children often stayed at home not just because of the temperature, but also because of the severely windy conditions. The wind would bite through clothes right to the bone. Breaks at school were also dependent on the outside temperature. It decided whether children remained indoors or went outside. Usually the minus twenty-five degree temperature was the cut off point. In contrast to the harsh winter outside, comfortably heated classrooms created an almost homely atmosphere.

Looking back to her school years, Arja admits that she was neither an outstanding student nor a tailender. "Instead I mostly achieved average marks; although I managed to be a well-behaved student at least. Science subjects were not my strong point. When it came to selecting foreign languages beside the compulsory Swedish and English, the choice was between French and German.

"At the time, our school didn't have a French teacher and with regard to the German language, a number of people told me, "German is too difficult." What makes a subject difficult? I thought to myself, isn't everything difficult in the beginning when we don't know much about the subject? As well as Latin, I took the plunge for German anyway, not knowing then that this language would turn out to become more important in my life than my mother tongue of Finnish. I lived from 1967 on in other parts of the world. This would be the pattern for the rest of my life. My future husband happened to live in Germany and the conversation in our home in later years ended up being German."

Later visits to Finland were more of a family homecoming. Arja never made any serious attempts with her own children to establish a firm footing in her country of origin. This was possibly because once she had a taste of other countries and their warmer climates, life in

Finland couldn't compare. Her new life started in Germany and went then to Africa, South America and Australia. The Finnish language eventually died out in the family especially with the children. Even though Arja would speak to them in Finnish, they responded more and more in the current language of the country in which they were living at the time.

A break with Finland was unavoidable since Arja's life as an adult continued outside of Finland. It can never be suggested that we lose something in life by adjusting to conditions of other countries and their people. In order to win something, one has always to give away a little of one's own.

Language lessons at school helped very little in practicing a foreign language. As a stay in another country, especially during early school years, was out of reach for most Finnish children, reading books and later, writing letters helped to establish contacts with students in England, Germany and beyond. Those letter correspondences to students in other countries gave the school lessons a more lively substance, over and above the books.

While Arja resolutely moved through her school years, there were incidents, which exemplified her attitude and skills. Arriving home from school one day she excitedly told her mum, "Mum, the music teacher told me today, my singing went off the notes." Arja strongly believed that it was a good performance until her mum gently set her right with a smile, "We both know that you like music and you try your best to improve on it; keep going and don't be afraid, because no master ever fell out of the sky."

"*Cats and dogs with their mewing and howling could have competed with my very own song efforts. In my defence, nobody is good at everything. Therefore, music remained for me a field in which I paid only the minimum attention, making sure to mix with others during singing to avoid being singled out.*

"*From my early school days, it is worth mentioning the fact that students learned by heart all sorts of text of any length, some Finnish subjects as well as religion, even before having learned to read or write. The obvious benefit out of it emerged only in later years when my memory in particular proved to have a lasting strength. The skill of intense concentration was also still evident. Today nobody could deny, at the beginning of the second Millennium, these areas of schooling leave much to be desired."*

"With technology advancing, a home telephone became more common in Finnish homes during 1957. It was more natural than anything else that children in particular wanted to find out more about it. My younger sister didn't worry much that her talking on the phone was difficult for others to understand. In the case of Tysse being away from the phone when it rang, Raija would pick up the phone. She would wait until the operator of that time asked for the wanted connection.

"Raija found out very quickly that instead of physically going across to the neighbours, the phone connected her easier and quicker with her playmates. The operator on the other side received instead of a number, a request for 'naabuliin' (neighbour), which miraculously sparked a connection to the right neighbours every time. Sympathy for children must have brought this connection together. In the end, everybody in town knew, when 'naabuliin' turned up on the phone, it was Raija wanting to talk to the neighbour's kids. Mum actually heard about the calls from somebody and had a good laugh."

Just like the larger community in those days, advancing progress in Finland did not necessarily lead to a better understanding. Also in Finland, people became more preoccupied with their own lives the further technology advanced. Raija's funny telephone game encouraged others to keep a more open, down-to-earth view of human contact and not shut this contact down because of technological progress.

School in these times was compulsory up to the age of eighteen. Finland had already recognized the benefit of a general education for its population at a very early stage. It developed over time the single public system for all, which internationally puts it into a leading position with countries like Taiwan. Irresolution in a child's school life can, in some cases, lead to the development of individual personality traits while at the same time a reduced attention towards school. This happened with Arja when she was ten and her mum sent her on a summer holiday again to the grandparents in Middle Finland. This time however she stayed with them and attended school in Nokia.

This change worked for the better in Arja's life. A modern school was burnt to the ground during one year. However, other teachers and new schoolmates helped initiate a new start for her. All classes in Finland were mixed; preparing boys and girls in an educational environment that was as good as the best in the world.

Finland doesn't believe in educational segregation for the purpose of a so-called better education. Shouldn't teachers determine the quality of their teaching and not a selective environment? Finns sympathized from early on with the Reformist movement of the Protestant religion. This led to Protestantism becoming the almost exclusive religion of the country.

The Finnish reformer Michael Agricola, in cooperation with Martin Luther, also comprehensively wrote of the religion. This led to religion, education and the language developing in close proximity. The people of Finland lived in a naturally close neighbourhood, which supported common goals and securing the Finnish identity throughout centuries of foreign occupation. Being able to read the Catechism properly was, from early on, a precondition for community consent to marriage.

Arja's grandfather still maintained rather proudly that he needed only two weeks of attending a school to know what he needed and to receive the seal of an approval for his marriage. He liked to point out, "Life is our best school." From the distance of time, it is necessary to add today, "If we continue to learn from it."

The school in Nokia was about twenty minutes by bus from Arja's grandparents' home. A short distance from the house, the bus picked her up and returned her in the afternoon on school days during the week. Her life with her grandparents went quite steadily as she approached the final classes before matriculation. To reach the marks for matriculation, every student had to work extremely hard after school. There were no more excuses for not bringing out one's best; in fact, it became the order of the day.

Through an International Correspondence Youth Organisation, Arja received addresses from England, Germany, Italy, Turkey, former Rhodesia, even from as far away as New Zealand. These were written in the foreign languages of Swedish, English and German. Writing letters was a good way of practicing, in writing, what school lessons and book reading had prepared her for. On certain days, the postman delivered more outside letters during a week to my grandparents' address than the week had days. It even happened that an address was either not complete or in some cases even missing and still the letters found their way into the right letterbox. This was due mainly to the fact that the postman very soon knew who was receiving so many letters from outside Finland.

Very often, the first letter from a new address revealed unexpected questions such as one Italian penpal, who asked Arja whether she was blond. Writing back that her hair was long and dark, no further letter arrived from this address. Apparently, Italians have a special liking for blond maidens. On another occasion, the Austrian penpal from Vienna became upset because Arja would not jump straight into an agreement with him to be his new foreign girlfriend. Nevertheless, she could exchange letters with enough others. Information on how they lived came from as far away as, for instance, the former Rhodesia or New Zealand. One penpal, Lynne, lived on a farm in Zimbabwe with her parents. They grew tobacco and maize on their property, which was one hour's drive outside the town of Bullawayo. This name sounded incredibly exotic in Arja's imagination. Lynne wrote that every school day during the week, the school bus picked up children from the countryside early in the morning, returning them late in the afternoon from the school in Bullawayo. The better-situated farmers, to whom Lynne didn't count, sent their children to boarding school during school time. For this 'privilege', they had to pay considerable fees.

Arja also learned, for the first time, that there were places on earth where summer reigns all year around. The only change was from a wet season during summer into a dry weather period during winter. In the southern hemisphere, the seasons of the year were the opposite of Finland. There they didn't know about the biting cold of winter.

Pictures arrived showing the natural environment and the wildlife in Lynne's country - zebras, lions, elephants, the mighty Victoria Falls, dense rainforests, and vast lush, agricultural land of a size not known in Finland. Like Arja, Lynne had to share the family work life on the farm before and after school as well as on weekends. School and work on the farm there went hand in hand from an early age.

Soon, Arja had friends from all over the world. "It didn't take long for pictures, especially from Africa and New Zealand, to decorate the walls of my room in my grandparents' house. My dreams from that time grew wings, which took me to Africa, the Americas and Pacific Oceania. From New Zealand, I received images of breathtaking mountainous regions, fire -spitting snow laden volcanoes, projecting sharp and high into the sky along with tranquil, lush green countryside of vineyards and grazing sheep. A record of Maori music transported me into a Pacific paradise. How beautiful the world must be!

"A deep longing must have captured me already in those early years of my life. People's lives in so many different parts of the world preoccupied me. Quicker than I could ever have thought, news from my New Zealand penpal Gwynne, of North Palmerston, brought me down to earth on hearing how life can sometimes treat us even in its early stages. Gwynne was a few years older than I, and already studying archaeology. She had been happily engaged to her fiancé. As she wrote to me, life for her was at its best until suddenly a fatal car accident involving her fiancé brutally changed all this. The first time I became aware in my life of how lucky I must have been so far, having been spared such an ordeal."

At that time, not much was available apart from books and the occasional film showing images from other distant countries and how people lived there. Everything was still far away, much further than in later years when tourism reached all corners of the world.

CHAPTER 4

Going Away From Finland

The nearest place to which Arja could pay a visit in the not too distant future was England. Something must have diverted her at that time from performing to the expectations of the teachers at school. As a result, she was given the 'opportunity' at least once in her school life to repeat a class. Feeling bad about it, Arja directed her mind away from school rather than intensifying a growing rift at home.

One day a totally unexpected incident helped her cause, when a woman customer spoke to Arja's grandmum in the grocery shop. She said her daughter had come to make a friend in England through letter exchanges. Arja overheard this conversation while listening undetected from the stairway that leads up into the house. After grandmum had told her story about Arja's penpals from around the world, she mentioned that Arja also had a penpal in England. As the woman left the shop, Arja hurried out to catch up with her to find out where she lived.

The next day after school, Arja went to this address. Here she exchanged with the woman's daughter, the news that the letters brought from other countries. Seija, the other daughter said that she was going to see her penpal in England in the coming summer. The idea appealed to Arja and she too decided to have a break from school and head to

England. Hopes were high that she would pick up the language she had failed at in class. On first hearing the plans, Arja's aunt couldn't help but exclaim, "How dare you want to go away instead of first repeating your class!"

However, nobody could change the young and stubborn mind of a strong willed girl; at least she had some support from mum and grand mum, who outnumbered the aunt's reservations. The day of Arja's first adventure leading her outside Finland couldn't come quickly enough for her. It was 1964 and she had made contacts in England with the help of Seija. A nursing home at Bromley, Kent, accepted her written application to attend a six-week, nursing course for elderly people in the home. When summer holidays came up, nothing could stop Arja wanting this experience of visiting a foreign country.

Sound preparation had to precede the trip. Firstly, there was the acquisition of a suitcase, which took all Arja's belongings for this journey away from home. Fortunately, she could still carry it on her own. The first leg of the trip was by boat to Stockholm in Sweden. Arja recalls the farewell scene.

"Mum and everybody else I knew in my hometown had come to the farewell at the landing place of Turku harbour. Only then did I feel the magnitude of my decision in front of people who cared about me, wishing me to go away well, but also to return safely. It nearly came to a heart-breaking scene, watching mum's tears roll down her cheeks despite her happiness. Once I arrived in the ship's labyrinthine corridors, I was simply stunned at how many people had come on board the ship. They couldn't all be going to England I thought, while searching for my seat number on one of the passenger decks."

Shortly after leaving the quay, the ship made its way through many magnificent little islands emerging out of the sea along the southwest corner of Finland. In the summer month of early July, the sun reigned almost all day on to shimmering ocean passages. This silently reflected peace in forest places, which struggled to hang on to the many granite formations growing out of the seabed.

The outpost islands of Ahvenanmaa were the last sight of Finnish territory. The ship lifted anchor from its capital Mariehamn in the middle of the night. It was not in complete darkness. Some daylight remained hovering at the northern horizon only to turn into full daylight again two hours into the new day. The ship's further passage to Stockholm was uneventful and soon Swedish land rose out of the Baltic Sea between islands.

During the voyage, the sea remained calm; likewise, the weather was warm and sunny. Arja was happy to have the company of her school friend, Seija, with whom this holiday break in England had been jointly organized. It had taken a period of a couple of months before their actual departure. Together, the girls felt much stronger and safer, visiting foreign soil for the first time. A test of their Swedish school knowledge awaited them immediately after leaving the ship in Stockholm. A bus took them to Central Station from where the train continued the journey. This indicated to the girls that their request in Swedish must have been correct.

However, at the railway station kiosk, a woman couldn't help saying, "You must be from Finland the way you talk Swedish." Not being satisfied with this, she continued excitedly in a way that made the girls leave her and go somewhere else for their shopping. There are always people around upsetting others by doing nothing better than spreading their anger about something often insignificant. All Arja and Seija wanted to do was to learn about other people and other places.

A long railway journey lay ahead throughout the whole of southern Sweden. Then, they would have to go across to Denmark on board a ship. Then the train continued on the European mainland after the mighty 'bird-flight bridge' crossing from Fehmarn Island. The further the train continued into mainland Europe, the more frequently settlements could be seen. The second night of the journey ended in Hock Van Holland, near Rotterdam, from where a ferryboat took the budding explorers across the Channel to England, to the northeast of London.

In Holland, Arja and Seija had to communicate in English, as they had no knowledge of Dutch at all. Most people in the crowd waiting for admission on to the big ferry were English citizens anyway, returning from a stay on the mainland. English helped them in Holland to get on the right boat to England. People here must have been used to travelling, as they were forthcoming and understood how it must be for young travellers in a foreign country. The ship was loaded too with passenger cars and trucks in its hull, making it almost full. In the early twilight of the third day in transit, the ship lifted anchor heading out into the English Channel under a misty, rainy sky.

The girls were incredibly tired from all the sitting in the train and waiting for the ship to leave. It was only natural they were ready for sleep soon after having secured a seat on one of the inner decks. Luggage and personal belongings were kept close so it was less likely anything would be lost. Two travellers can help each other see more and, as a result, travel safer. Once the ship had left the shelter of the coast to steam into the open Channel, waves suddenly caused the boat to start rolling so that a much-needed snooze was disrupted. Travelling on a ship can sometimes turn into a memorable experience especially when people experience 'stomach problems'. Fortunately, neither Arja nor Seija experienced any seasickness.

Because of the poor weather conditions, the ship's restaurant hardly saw any guests. This at least helped in terms of saving a bit of money that wasn't spent on food. In addition, hardly anybody spoke a word during this wavering voyage, which fortunately lasted only a few hours. Then the ship reached the relatively calm waters in the protection of the Thames bay. Nobody anticipated the sea to be as rough as it was but once calm had returned, closer to Harwich destiny, life on board the ship quickly returned to normal and everybody started to get prepared to disembark.

The weather on arrival lived up to what is said about the English weather - drizzly and rainy. With both feet firmly back on land, Arja and Seija followed the instructions they had received on the ship about how to get to London by public transport. Buses in a nearby terminal waited to take people in all different directions. All the friends had to do was to make sure they boarded the right bus to London. People were quite friendly so the girls didn't feel like strangers in a foreign country.

The bus was fully loaded to the last seat with other passengers off the ship. It delivered everyone right into the centre of the huge city of London. Long before leaving the bus again though, the girls saw dense housing estates surrounding the city. The closer the bus came to its destination, the more traffic there was. The legendary red double-decker buses moved around the busy inner city with its countless high-rise buildings and places of interest.

While driving along the mighty river Thames, the famous Big Ben tower stood side by side with the Parliament buildings. In the not too far distance, the Royal Palaces could be seen. On the way, a number of historical as well as modern looking bridges all led to the other side of London, which continued relentlessly in a sea of rich ornamental facades on many buildings.

In these early morning hours, a grey sky concealed the sunny images of this pulsing metropolis. It was the first time that either girl had seen so many houses, so much motor vehicle traffic and such constantly moving streams of people. Despite tiredness, all these new impressions and levels of noises alerted them enough to keep them awake for the time being.

Trafalgar Square-London, Arja, 1964

At Trafalgar Square, everybody had to get off the bus. Not much time was left to reach Bromley before the end of the day. On the way to the nearest underground station, Nelson's Column briefly attracted attention. Then, the endless wooden staircases leading under the city, introduced the girls to a different traffic world. Here, large numbers of people rushed downwards on one side of the wide stairway while an apparently similar number on the other side moved in the opposite direction. Everybody pushed by in a rush.

The ticket for the bus trip to London was included in their travel documents, but after that, the girls had to buy their own tickets. They had to listen carefully to the instructions to change at Victoria Station to the train that would carry them to Bromley. It was not so much the ticket, but the money comprising their change that confused them. The coins particularly puzzled them so that they had no clue of how much change they held in their hands after having handed over only a one-pound note. However, this could be sorted out later as the U-Tube, as the underground is called in London, was just about to arrive.

Arja recalls how they coped with all these transport issues. "Together with everybody else, we rushed the last steps down to the platform, where the tube waited already. My friend Seija followed a few steps behind me. The moment I had entered the rail compartment right in front of us, the two sliding doors shut decisively behind me, leaving my friend behind on the platform.

"I was frightened beyond description. Seija had my ticket as well as hers and what would happen when the inspector wanted to see my ticket? Will we get lost now? All I could do was get out of the train at the next station. Here I was, lost and alone, not knowing what to do, waiting to be reunited with my friend. At first, I did nothing but wait. Surprisingly this paid off quicker than I could have even dared to hope for. After a while, my friend came down the stairs to the platform where I waited. What a relief! Nothing could stop us from embracing and losing instantly any fear of getting lost in this city jungle. The next train arrived and we made sure to enter together without any delay or the slightest distance from each other.

"Just before dusk on our third travelling day, the train delivered us on this last leg of our journey. A call from the public phone box connected us with the nursing home. The woman on the other side welcomed us very openly and told us to stay where we were so that somebody could pick us up. We had arrived well and truly outside of London. Here there was much less traffic and fewer people, more like a country town.

"Shortly after, a car arrived at the station front. No other car had turned up so it must have almost certainly been the pick-up service from the nursing home. The gentleman who stepped out of the car addressed with an inviting gesture, "You must be the two Finnish guests waiting to be picked up by the nursing home. I am Arthur, the driver of the local nursing home; you are both welcome. After your long journey from Finland, you certainly must also be a bit tired. I'll put the luggage for you in the back of the car. What is your name? Please, take a seat. Your names are certainly different from our English names. I only hope I remember them. We have only a few minutes' drive; the matron Alice is waiting for you.

"Our response to this friendly introduction was rather shy and short, "Thank you for picking us up." The day of our arrival in England was a Saturday. Despite three days' and two nights' travel on ship, train and bus, everything finally went to plan. All we needed was a rest and the matron followed our wish without hesitation *not spending extra time with us in the reception. Everybody else in the nursing home received us in an emphatically friendly way; we didn't feel like foreigners having to try hard to communicate in a foreign language. On the contrary, everything just seemed natural that we had arrived and straight away become part of a bigger family, caring for the elderly in this place of support."*

Lennard Hospital-Bromley/Kent-England,1964

Mrs. Smith, the matron, was shorter than everybody else in the reception area at the time. Nevertheless, she made her presence known through a stout appearance and her decisive regimen. The nearest female staff to her received clear orders, "Bring our new staff members to the home ward across the road and show them their room. Tomorrow morning after a good rest, I'll see you both here in the reception again. Ask the receptionist Ann for me and I'll take care of you. By the way, my name is Karen. I'd better write down your names before I turn around forget them. Your names, Seija and Arja sound very harmonious. Tell my ward nurse May what you need on the way to your rooms. See you again tomorrow."

May was fairly new here too and came from Jamaica to be trained in nursing. This was the first time in the girls' lives that they had even spoken to a person with such a beautiful chocolate skin colour. Her hair was black as coal and she smiled in a friendly way with her clear, wide-open, deep dark eyes as she talked to Arja and Seija. No wonder they had received such a friendly reception; they were not the only foreigners in the place. Arja instantly learned how people from different parts of the world could so naturally communicate. Kindness was the key when reaching out to other people in a surprisingly common understanding. People from very different parts of the world had come together to learn and work, communicate and live together.

This was something nobody had told the two girls at school or at home. At that time in 1964, it was something they had to find out by going out into the world to meet other people. Life outside their country and home worked somewhat differently to what had been described. The new experiences turned around Arja's attendance at school positively after her homecoming. For now, she attended the first week of lessons in the nursing home on caring for the needy elderly. Once they were declared fit to help the many elderly of the nursing home, work began for real. The majority of the residents were women, some having reached very old ages, whereas others battled a disability from earlier on. All this work was mind-blowing for two young girls from the relatively sheltered environment in Finland.

Because Arja came from stable and happy living conditions, she was astounded to learn of all the difficulties other people had encountered. People, whose lives had brought, during the course of years, problems of different natures, now needed the help of others. Daily care for the elderly differed in levels of demand as allocations were shifted between nursing patients. Some of the patients were more independent than others. When the sun smiled occasionally over the English sky, a visit outside among the carefully established gardens rewarded patients and carers for an hour or so. Most of the time, the more independent patients needed only basic attention with little help when moving around in the nursery.

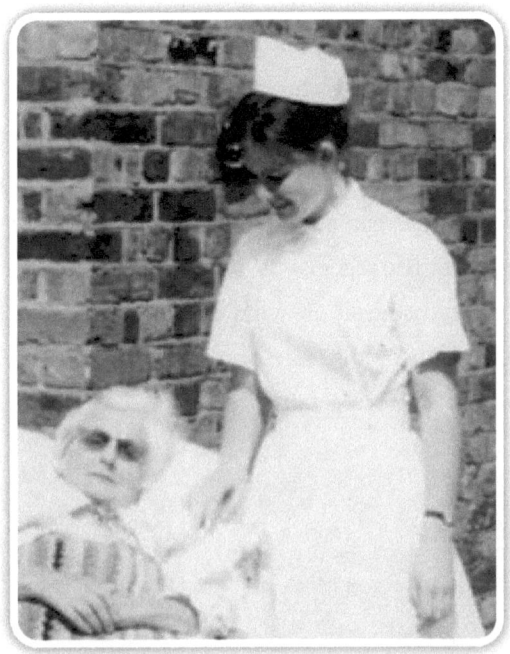

Lennard Hospital, Arja with patient

However, there were also cases that needed constant help, even for the most basic necessities like eating, changing clothes, toilet, cleaning and refreshing. Most of the time, two carers helped, as moving immobilized patients was too difficult for one carer only. The six-day working week from Monday until Saturday was difficult but also had its rewards. Mrs. Stuart, one of Arja's regular patients, was truly grateful and happy after the lengthy work of refreshing her, newly refurbishing the bed and the wheel chair, serving meals and handing out her medical prescriptions. She engaged the staff in conversation, showing newborn joyfulness. Mrs. Stuart then forgot about her disabled condition and asked so many questions about the country of Finland, family, school, friends and what Finns like most. Regarding the latter, it was of course, sauna.

The girls' English became better by the day. The initial barriers of anxiety about speaking correctly, melted away, as they gradually gained confidence face to face with the indigent elderly. Arja learnt many things in her life at the home; the most important perhaps that life is not necessarily a contract for the better. Only with the help of others, some individual suffering can be eased, but we should never become complacent and take the good life for granted. Sometimes in a matter of moments, difficulties can change our lives. If we were to know when we were young, what life teaches us, would we be any better off? These were not the only discussions with nursing patients. Sunny breaks through a more often cloudy sky brought messages of hope through the windows to the suffering patients.

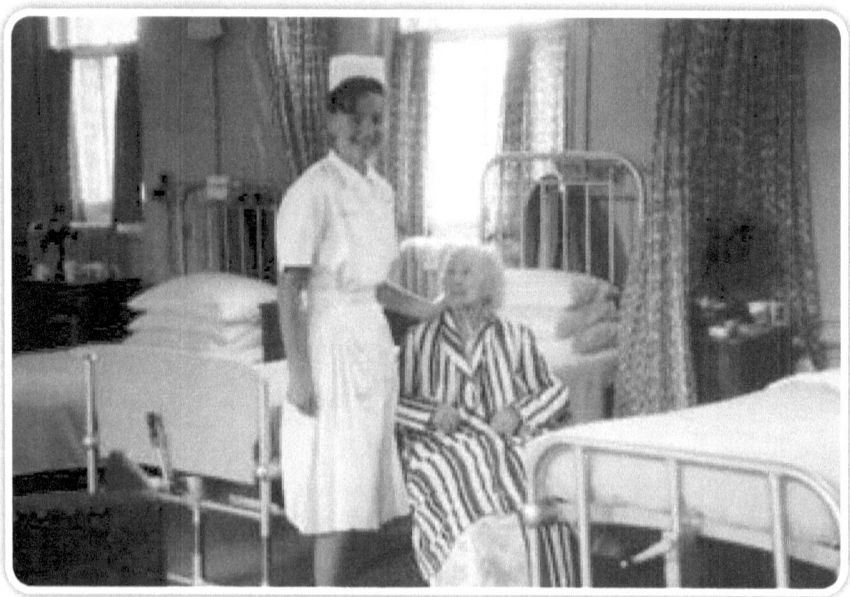

Arja with patient

The Larth Ward Staff-Lennard Hospital with patient

It was an unforgettable experience to see how so little could make such positive changes to disabled people's focus, moving it slightly towards a more positive outlook. Their conversation turned immediately away from expressing sorrow over their own conditions. Moreover, this was one of the many tasks of which nursing staff had to be aware in supporting the well being of patients. Medicine alone cannot achieve what it is supposed to without the broader help of the patient and all those people and things around them.

The spacious park, in which the scattered mansions of the nursing home lay, offered daily possibilities for a patient outing with the staff as soon as the weather came to the party. Patients, who were not able to walk, couldn't wait to be moved in wheelchairs along the alleys of the park where rosebuds and flowers smiled in red and pink to the ones who looked at it. Green English lawn stretched between the garden beds, brown freshly furrowed soil shimmering through in spots added an earthy scent to a mixture of flowers. The grass continued into islands of wood, interrupted by dense hedges, thoroughly trimmed to look fresh in its varying greens. Some old grown trees bestowed silence upon the park.

There were also moments during a day when both patients and staff recuperated inside the house for the time being. Noises from busy roads didn't reach most areas of the park so that peace and silence added to everybody's comfort. Often patients didn't talk at all while collecting undisturbed impressions, which they freely exchanged on the days they were banished indoors.

Sunday was Arja's day off and during her six working weeks at the nursing home, only once did it happen that Seija had the same day off. On that day, sightseeing in London became the order of the day, as they didn't want to miss a little insight into what London had to offer during their stay. They were up earlier than on working days in order to catch the train to London. Where their first tube experience started, at Trafalgar Square, right in the centre of a busy London, Arja tells of their sightseeing day, which started without any hiccups this time.

"Keeping close to each other, my friend Seija and I started out on an exceptionally warm Sunday at the end of June in 1964. We set out on an inner city tour, partly on foot. We were anxious to see how much could be squeezed into one day's program. Some pedestrians must have felt hot already early in the day, because the big round fountain at Trafalgar Square attracted quite a number of people to sit on the stone ring edge and cool their feet in the fountain's basin. At the same time, they were also catching some of the fine mist, which a light breeze carried through the air. Hundreds of pigeons flocked around the people, knowing from experience that bread and biscuit crumbs would reward them for their persistence.

"We returned, however, to our sightseeing program for which one day seemed a tight measure. In order to see something of the variety London has to offer, we split our day into a double-decker bus tour to gain an overall impression and other venues around London. We planned to see what else could be visited until the late afternoon, when we had booked a visit to the theatre near Trafalgar Square. It would be the late hours of Sunday before we headed home. The matron knew about our program and accepted our returning later than usual.

"Starting from Trafalgar Square, we tried to remember what we knew about England's hero Nelson and the name of Trafalgar. The 1815 English victory over the French-Spanish fleet in Trafalgar, Southern Spain was under the command of vice admiral Horatio Viscount Nelson. It was then that he was fatally wounded, rising nevertheless to hero status.

"On the top deck of a typically red London bus, we took a seat watching all the cars and pedestrians. They didn't disturb our tour or many of those fabulous sites, which make up London. Undisrupted, the bus found its way through dense traffic and people crossing everywhere. Many of the people were dressed in official black suits, tight, upright, white shirt collars, keeping the heat well and truly locked in. Others were dressed casually, which actually better suited the warm weather of the day. In their inclined position, the top louvers above the bus windows caught a breeze from outside, sending it through the heated cabin of the bus.

"As long as we were moving in traffic, relief from the heat came from outside. Stopping in traffic was not short enough to bring the heat back instantly. Everybody was talking about the obviously unusual heat of the day; nobody seemed to be prepared for it. We noticed this as the formally dressed pedestrians got on and off the bus. Their elegant image was very much spoilt by the sweat visibly running down their faces, stopping only where the collar was kept tight.

"Despite all this discomfort, people still waited patiently in perfectly aligned rows not only at bus stops but also in front of trains or public buildings. It appeared to me to be an attitude of patience, which reflected favourably on the necessary public discipline within a crowded place like London. On our tour with the bus, we passed many of London's best known attractions - Westminster Abbey (hosting English poet memorials), the grand Houses of Parliament, the famous bell tower of Big Ben, Buckingham Palace (guarded by the tall Royal Keepers in their black, upstanding fur caps, which must have given them a lot of discomfort in the heat), and Hyde Park. It surprised us with its size in the middle of London. The most novel aspect of the park was its legendary 'Speakers' Corner' where men and women equally, have been able to speak freely in front of a public audience every Sunday since 1866.

"It was surprising to find here, on one side, firm tradition and at the same time openness towards non-traditional expressions. The doors open to the world,

England must have adopted an open mind earlier to other expressions despite the strong maintenance of in-house traditions.

"Our bus made an inner-city round tour all the way to the Tower Bridge along the River Thames, passing on the way a number of other significant bridges, which connect both sides of London. Having returned to Trafalgar Square, we opted to visit at least two museums during the remaining daytime hours. The National Gallery, just next to Trafalgar Square exhibited well-known artwork from around the world.

"To include a visit to the British Museum, we took a taxi, trying to save some time for the museum visit. It needed plenty of time in order to see more than a rushed visit could deliver. The British Museum holds the most extensive library of England as well as Egyptian, Greek, and Roman historical collections. We saw the most controversial of these, the 'Parthenon Sculptures' from Athens.

"Days earlier, it had been arranged for us also to take in a theatre performance near Trafalgar Square. The comedy was called 'Mister Brown Comes Down the Hill' and our pre-bookings secured us a seat in the full house. The play amused everybody in the packed noble premises of the theatre. Famous performers secured the success of the evening in a splendid environment of antique fittings, to which everybody had come fashionably dressed.

"Velvet, purple-red seats with individual elbow rests spread upwards in circles, continuing along the sides and opposite the stage-platform to rise in niches to the ceiling. Everybody had an uninterrupted view from other seats in front. During the performance, every single word could be clearly heard thanks to the genuine rising circle layout of the theatre, where in reality nobody was too far away from the scene.

"With our entertainment over, it was time to head back to Bromley. This dictated when to take the tube and the train again. A city the size of London with its almost never-resting pulsing life makes you easily forget to take care of the basics like eating! On the way to the station, hunger registered with us for the first time. All day our eyes had absorbed so many delights that the stomach's voice had gone unheard. A quick snack was all we could take to the U-Tube to ensure we did not miss our return connection. In the end, it was hunger not fatigue that overcame us at the end of a solid sightseeing-day in London. Falling asleep would have been so easy, but to play it safe we kept each other awake by recalling our experiences of this day in London.

"Back in Bromley, waking up in time the next morning was a different kettle of fish. Luckily, Wanja and Fay, our two room colleagues, got us out of bed in time for the start of another working week. Our patients asked us about our London experience while a mountain of work still had to be done. Besides the work, conversations with patients were an excellent opportunity to practice our English. In only six weeks in England, I probably learnt more English than in all the years at school."

One could easily have asked the question, why had school been so far off track in preparing for life outside it. Surely, school should work on preparation, which is meant to facilitate the learning process in life after school. The girls' time in England flew by, because the nursing home kept everybody busy, which in a way was good. Arja learnt to speak the English language better, especially in communicating directly with local people, but she also learnt that other young women from even further away than Finland, have taken this step to go out and learn how people in other countries live.

The quintessence was, people in other countries usually express the same wishes and hopes. It is only languages and customs that create the distance between them as long as one side hasn't learnt enough about the other one. Whoever goes out to learn from there, will make friends everywhere. Ignorance towards others' conditions has been the biggest hurdle in people's peaceful ambitions.

While still in England, Arja thought to contact her pen friend in Wales, northwest of London. This, however, didn't eventuate as her letter reached them too late, only the day before departure from England. The response received in the letter was very kind; the whole family of Arja's penpal wanted to pick her up and invited her to spend some time with them. Unfortunately, this couldn't happen as the time before departure again required some proper preparation. Arja and Seija had arrived more or less with sunshine in England and unbelievably, left with sunshine too. England must have kept in store its sunny side especially for them.

They had many good memories to take with them after a farewell party with all the staff and patients. Arja surpassed herself by delivering a speech for the first time in her life, even if it was a short one. She thanked everybody for the kindness and attention she and Seija had received. Even the little matron couldn't hide a tear rolling down her cheek. Indeed, hard shells often contain a soft core.

The big departure took place from London harbour, where a Russian freighter also took passengers on board on her journey, anchoring too in Helsinki, Finland. The driver from the nursing home who had picked up the girls six weeks before gave them both a hearty hug, the best sign they could have received from a family. In addition, despite their stay of only six weeks with the nursing home at Bromley, they had received acceptance and the care of a bigger family.

Arja pointed out, "I must have turned, at least partly, into a different person after my first time away from home. I was starting to understand better what life is all about. In the case of the innate family, we can easily become spoilt, not necessarily waking up in time to the challenges that lie ahead in our lives."

"Baschkiria" from London to Helsinki, 1964

The name of the Russian ship was 'Baschkiria'. The freighter ship was huge and therefore could offer cabins just like a passenger ship, only the fare was considerably cheaper. 'Baschkiria' made its voyage without interruptions through the Atlantic to the north, passing Denmark and Sweden through the Baltic Sea. It reached Helsinki, the capital of Finland, in only two days and two nights. Helsinki is located two hundred kilometres to the east of Arja's hometown of Turku.

Only a few other passengers occupied other cabins on the ship, while the ship's crew kept to themselves on other parts of the ship. It was only during the reception on the ship, that a Russian officer in stylish black uniform and white cap welcomed the passengers in English as well as in Russian. The silence on the ship during our passage must have been an indication that the Russians kept to themselves not only because of a language barrier. Vodka was also at that time the Russian wake-up call, which the girls didn't experience during the journey. Arja knew from home the role alcohol plays in the colder northern parts of Europe; it is almost an epidemic. Strict rules must have been in place on the ship as no sign of the 'Vodka-life' came to the attention of the young travellers.

CHAPTER 5

Priorities in Turku and Nokia

Arja's homecoming was very different from her departure. After disembarking in Helsinki and taking the train to Turku, she only later continued on the last leg to Nokia in Middle Finland. By the end of July, there was a still five weeks of school holiday before the new school year began in Nokia. Everything now looked different to Arja since having left this so familiar place at home. Her Mum didn't fail to express her own observations, "Arja, you are different from before leaving home. I hope it will turn out for you better." And indeed, it did. From that time on, Arja looked at school with a changed view, instantly moving from a poor performer to a top performer, not only in the study of the English language, but overall.

Life after returning from England held something in store at home, too. Just when one wondered, what could be done next for the remainder of the holidays, Arja's father, Petteri, turned up out of the blue with a bunch of international race car drivers. Despite Petteri not being able to speak one word of another language, he managed to invite these drivers from Sweden, England and Germany into the home for a big dinner with plenty of beer all around.

Arja was given the task of mediation between the four nationalities. The beer definitely helped the guests to feel at home in Finland and Arja was kept busy as everybody began to open up and talk. Translating constantly into four languages during this Saturday event proved to be a new challenge for Arja, but it was one, which she enjoyed. Mum especially expressed her pride by realizing the benefits of at least one family member having been able to converse with people from abroad. Arja was certainly a front-runner in learning to deal with people from outside her own country.

Generally speaking, visiting other countries both far and wide was then still fairly rare. People's ideas, as far as travelling abroad, had only just started to develop. Arja's stay in England happened on the basis of employment and her choice of travelling was decided on the basis of economy. Her trip was governed by tight budget planning. As often occurs in life, once one opportunity arises so too does another.

Arja clearly remembers the next event and recounts the story. "In a shopping centre of Turku, a Japanese medical doctor had tried to find out to whom he could speak in English. A lady, who knew our family, rang us at home, putting the gentleman on the phone with us. Mum took the call, quickly handing over the phone to me by explaining, "Arja, there is somebody talking English for you." Indeed the gentleman spoke English fluently. "I am from Tokyo in Japan and have worked as a doctor in a hospital in Denmark for the last twelve months. I just arrived in Finland and tried to find somebody I can converse with in English, as I have no knowledge of the Finnish language whatsoever. I am calling with the kind assistance of a supermarket employee. You obviously understand and can speak English. Could we meet in town? How far away are you?"

"In response, I said, "Could you please wait a moment so I can discuss with my mother how we can best help you?" I hurriedly explained to mum the situation, 'There is a Japanese gentleman stuck in the centre of Turku looking for somebody to talk to.' Mum answered straight away, 'Tell the gentleman our address. The lady in the shopping centre can write it on a piece of paper for him which he can show to a taxi driver. Tell him also that he is welcome as our guest.'

"Said and done! The message was passed via the phone and it remained to be seen, who of the two parties was most nervous. First, we doubted that the gentleman would turn up at our place at all. But as time went by, a car stopped in front of our house and out of it emerged a well-dressed gentleman in a black suit holding a travel bag in one hand. As the gentleman approached our gate, mum sought a place to hide behind me, pushing me in front so that I faced our new foreign guest first. It was obvious our guest came from another part of the world other than from a neighbourhood of Finland. Referring to the telephone call, the gentleman introduced himself first to me, 'I called half an hour earlier from the city. My name is Yutaka Yamasaki. I am from Japan and like to see more of Scandinavia, especially Finland. Thank you for your kind invitation which I am very pleased to accept.'

Yamazaki visit from Japan

"Because it was difficult remembering a foreign name, I gratefully received his visiting card, which produced the name in clear letters. However, half of the card showed Japanese lettering, which was something, which I couldn't relate at all. After slowly picking up the name from the card, I invited our guest into our house, 'Please come inside; my mother also wants to welcome you.' However, before setting foot across the entrance, the Japanese gentleman took off his shoes, placing them next to each other at the side of the house. Only then did he step forward in his socks. I learned that in Japan, people take their shoes off before entering a house, an obliging gesture, which honours every homemaker's efforts in keeping a home nice and clean.

"In the meantime, Mum was busy in the kitchen getting a quick homemade cake out of the oven for final placement on a tray, waiting on the table. The moment our guest came past the kitchen door, mum excitedly waved with one hand, dropping the cake out of the other hand. It fell straight onto the floor. Mum was embarrassed more than anything else, managing still to downplay the mishap with her words, "In Finland, we welcome people with a cake on the floor." Our visitor was not at a loss for joining in a mutual effort to place the cake back where it belonged by adding his comment, "A cake from the floor must be a better cake." Mum didn't need my translation; somehow she must have picked up the essence of his comment and everybody had a heartfelt laugh. The initial timidity had been brushed aside; the cake had become a wonderful mediator.

"By walking through the corridor of the house, the party reached the other side, the closed glass window veranda. My little sister curiously sneaked in from her room in the house, watching with special interest our guest who had come from so far away. When Mr. Yamazaki addressed her, her face turned bright red, as she couldn't respond in another language yet. Our guest knew however to give my sister her confidence back with the complimentary gesture of a handshake.

"Everybody had taken a seat on the veranda, judging by closer inspection the family cake, which had been picked up off the floor. During this occasion, Mr. Yamazaki also expressed his delight at experiencing the open spaces in this sparsely populated part of Northern Europe. "I was brought up in Tokyo which has three times the population of the whole of Finland. You don't have such a density of houses, people and traffic in Finland. I envy your freedom of living in a natural, pristine environment: no pollution, vast forested areas, many lakes and most of all the straightforward, friendly people. We know to appreciate this in Japan, because everything in our lives has become increasingly competitive in our so much denser society. We've already learnt to accept leaving very early in the morning to get to work in time and returning home only late in the day, in complete darkness. Many families meet on public transport, trying to spend some extra time together when not much time is left apart from the need to get enough sleep. In Tokyo, the vast majority of people cannot have houses and gardens like you have. Our progress in Japan is measured differently from your country. Therefore, it is so interesting to see how people live and work in other parts of the world.

"Tomorrow I am going to rent a car for a few days and would like to invite all of you to show me around your part of the country." Adding to his interesting comments, I said, 'We know somebody in town who rents cars. If you wish, we could organize it from here on behalf of you; it's only a phone call away. After we have cake and coffee, we can get the car organized for you and then perhaps go with our boat around the city via the many Baltic Sea inlets. We can stop on the numerous forested islands as often as we like. Our days in summer are almost entirely filled with daylight as you might have already realized. From 11pm until 2am, twilight takes over, sending the sun down near the horizon. Life in Finland during summer is enjoyed over most of the long daylight hours as during winter, we face the opposite with only a few hours of daylight.'

"Mum added to the conversation, 'Let's go on the boat as long as we have enough sunny hours left for the day; it's already past 6pm. We could also drop our guest in town near his hotel later on. It is located only a short distance off the Aurajoki river shores, which lead through the whole city. I am going to prepare a picnic basket that we can take with us. Is there anything special you would like us to take care of?' Translating this backwards and forwards to our visitor and then again to mum, Mr. Yamazaki exclaimed, 'I am quite happy to see what people in Finland like to eat. I will follow you.'

"My dad Petteri was not around home at the time, so mum and I took control of our outboard motorized boat, which anchored at the end of the garden on the wooden jetty leading into the initially shallow sea. We had not chosen the smaller, timber rowboat because it would take too much time moving around everywhere we wanted to go. The sun still stood high in the sky and a nice warm summer day promised us an enjoyable sightseeing tour on the many waterways around and in Turku. Some days it can turn fairly hot during the long sunny hours, especially before a storm builds on the horizon. Today, this wasn't going to happen, so that we could go out unconcerned about the weather. Our boat 'Margareta' had on board compulsory life jackets and floating rings besides other necessary equipment to run the boat. There was also basic fishing gear consisting of rods and one or two catching nets on a bar.

"Once we left and were moving more into the open, calm water, we switched the motor off from time to time and enjoyed the views across to the city or the small granite islands. These stuck out of the seawater with the persistent Finnish forest grabbing a hold everywhere on shore. While floating calmly in the water, we could sometimes see fish with the naked eye. They came closer to the surface to snatch dancing insects from the air. Our boat trip went to everybody's satisfaction; there was no rush or unexpected incidents.

"Watching the islands from the water, there were only a few other boats visible here and there. Parts of the city could be seen and more undulating land of green forests, green meadows, and canola fields blossoming bright yellow. Closer to the city, harbour installations could be seen where the city river 'Aurajoki' runs into the Baltic Sea. The movements of big ships had to be watched in terms of 'passing by' rules. 'Goliath' has right of way over everybody else. Past the harbour, only small boats like ours resumed traffic upstream into the heart of Turku city.

"Close to 10pm with the sun nearing the horizon, our boat anchored after the first bridge opposite 'Michaeli Church', a landmark in the city built of solid, rocky blocks. It had a sharply pointed bell tower reaching high into the sky. It was here that we said good-bye to Mr. Yamazaki who had only a short walk to his hotel. We three remaining on the boat, mum, my sister and I, had to make sure to get home while the daylight lasted.

"The next day our Japanese guest turned up in front of our house with a flash Volvo passenger car, so precisely on time that we could have set our clock by his arrival. Mum told me to let Mr. Yamazaki know of how much his punctuality was appreciated to which he responded, 'Punctuality is what Queens deserve.' Mum complimented him on his politeness, which became a good translation exercise for me.

"On the trip, we took an assortment of picnic foods, put together out of our kitchen stock. Everybody's purse needed careful treatment at that time, so there were no extravagances. Every bit of food that the individual could provide out of his or her own supplies helped to keep the budget healthy. Our Japanese visitor fully agreed too that we take our Finnish food with us. 'What Japan has in common with Finland,' he suggested, 'is to have fish and veggies on the family table. We also like to eat healthy.' In our case, the fish was left at home, as no portable cooling bag was available. However, there was coffee in a thermos flask, bread, biscuits, smoked ham, newly collected apples and a specialty of strawberries, blueberries, and cranberries, each in its own sealed clay jar. With all this, our tour could proceed.

"In the city, we stopped in order to see all the worthwhile sights first: the old castle with its museum of art collections overlooking the harbour, and the craft museum in the historical part of the city, which was spared during history only later to be consumed by fire. One could see here a lady in traditional costume spinning wool to thread on a spinning wheel or a blacksmith heating red hot steel bars in a forge, forming them with skilled hands into a useful tool over an anvil.

"The University district appeared very small compared to that of Tokyo, Mr. Yamazaki exclaimed but added, 'It must be nice studying in an environment where students and teachers can still work closely together whereas in Tokyo, this is an en masse service.' I hurried to mention that it was my firm intention to enter this University of Turku, which by the way, is also the longest established one in the country going back into the sixteenth century. 'What do you want to study?' Mr. Yamazaki questioned me.

"I wish I knew exactly, because I've to finish school first as the final examinations at school determine an enrolment not only into University but which discipline to choose from. Terms of entering University are very strict and fussy; I do hope to get there.

"It was decided unanimously that we had spent enough time in the city. The weather was sunny and warm with hardly any clouds in the sky, promising that the weather would continue like that. Our summerhouse outside the city became the perfect destination for a picnic. On arrival, our Japanese visitor could not believe what he saw. He found it difficult to believe that people in Finland had a choice of a house in or near the city in addition to a spacious setup in the country.

"In Tokyo we struggle for each living space, no matter how small it might be."

"While mum prepared a luncheon inside the house, the timber rowboat anchored in front of the sauna hut, took the three of us out to try our luck catching fish. We would have liked some fish for our table. Luck was on our side. In half an hour, the simple fishing rod caught two good-sized perches, and a number of little sardines.

"This is a real holiday. We call in Japan, what you are living, a holiday paradise and not in an industrial hub like Tokyo. You don't know how lucky you are."

"I couldn't restrain myself from adding to our guest's obliging remarks, 'Wait until winter arrives in two months; then paradise looks very different.'

"In the north of Japan, for instance on the island of Hokkaido, we also know what winter is like. Your summer with its long sunny days can compensate you so much for the long winter."

"With our catch back on land, our Japanese guest surprised us by using short Finnish sentences. "Where did you learn this?" I had to ask. "Japanese is as difficult or as easy as your Finnish language, depending which way one wants to look at it. I like to learn something difficult like your language. However, Finnish and Japanese are not total strangers to each other. We have a dialect in the north of Hokkaido, which has some similarity to the sounding of the Finnish language. Could there be some connection between the languages way back in history?"

'The catchword 'sauna' prompted us to introduce our guest into a Finnish sauna but later after lunch, because heating wood to the right temperature needed a fair bit of time. Sauna apparently is something familiar for most Japanese, as they have a strong tradition in bathing after sauna. Meanwhile, boiled fresh potatoes and freshly caught fried fish contributed to the main course of our meal, which was followed by a basket full of other tasty food. Not to downgrade everybody's efforts for the meal, the truth still remained - hunger has always been the best cook!

'Looking at nature's unspoiled 'kingdom' of Southern Finland seemed to have impressed the Japanese visitor. Courtesy of meeting differences in Finnish and Japanese culture, the sauna was placed entirely at our guest's liking. After sauna and swimming, nobody could miss the polite notes of Mr. Yamazaki in Finnish, "Olen kuin uudestisyntynyt (I am like a new-born)." Mum on her part couldn't think of a better 'thank you'. Playing badminton under the veranda, and resting in a deck chair with a picture book of Finland, helped pass the time in the afternoon in warm, sunny weather conditions.

"Time marched on to late afternoon and told us to move on if we wanted to see more of the immediate environs of southwest Finland. Naantali to the west was less than one hour's drive away, prompting us to also look at the small village as a contrast to the city of Turku. On our way, typical landscapes of green meadows between ripe yellow, brownish cornfields alternated with bright yellow field spots of canola, again limited by dark green pine forest stocks. The country road wound across hillocks not carrying much of the city traffic any more. Peace lays in the country. Haycocks waited in grassy fields for the summer sun to dry them, before being brought in for winter storage.

"Naantali goes back centuries in history, displaying a preserved town image beside its facade of modern buildings. In the lower part of the town, water inlets share the space between old timber houses with cobbled roads, all kept in good nick. An old windmill attached to a massive tower, still operational, told its own story from connections throughout history. Further south, the 'Hanse Cities' were located along the Baltic Sea coastline.

"The time of day and vanishing daylight warned us to return slowly to Turku, rounding off the day's excursion with an invitation from our Japanese guest to 'Sampalinna Restaurant'. I had named it, along with 'Kakola', the city's prison, as one of the best places to visit besides the other known places of Turku. People think this is a joke, but very soon, somebody will find out the excellence of "Sampalinna", a well-kept old white timber restaurant- featuring balconies along the river Aurajoki, peacefully located in the middle of the city.

"Our 'glad rags' had also come with us from our morning start, setting here the tone for a mutual 'thank you' and farewell to our Japanese visitor. Mum had, as a special treat, organized a musician who performed for us with the Finnish zither-like 'kantele' while we dined exclusively on one of the restaurant balconies with views across the river. On the opposite bank, colourful boats of varying sizes and outfits patiently waited at anchor.

"I'll take all these memories back to Japan and keep Finland always close to my heart. When you come to Japan, I promise to show you my country; you were so kind and open to me. Thank you for giving me so much of your attention. I propose now a toast to charming mother Tysse and her two daughters." The formality Mr. Yamazaki had chosen was that of a world-travelled gentleman. For my part, I learnt that he, who opens himself to people from other countries can only enrich himself, while cautiously adopting the so important knowledge of a human nature, which ultimately determines where we stand in life."

The family's sightseeing changed back to life's daily realities without transition. Arja's break from school in Nokia drew closer to an end in mid August. However, an incident of only minor importance happened before Arja left her hometown of Turku again. At the time, in 1964, Arja had turned nineteen years old. Contrary to her sister, she didn't take much notice of the opposite gender. Examples of her father's lifestyle and how it impacted especially on her mother had distanced Arja from contact with boys. She chose instead a walk with the dog in the surrounding fields rather than wasting time with needless chatter. At least this was how Arja thought at that stage of her life.

One particular neighbour's son, also nineteen, thought to stay uncompromisingly by Arja's side by following her for some time in the hope of earning her attention. Alas, this was not going to happen as she gave him a final rebuke when he followed her during an afternoon on the water. "Get out of my way and leave me alone." Arja knew this was not very kind, but in life, we do many things, which in hindsight serve our own ends. Kulervo, the boy in question, who Thysse had earlier helped to raise as a baby, didn't give up, telling Arja that he wanted to be her friend. Later in the day, he even came into the house and took a seat in front of the TV while everybody watched a documentary on wildlife in Africa.

Television then was only recently introduced in Finland. Mainly the family would watch it for a few hours in the afternoon. Petteri, Arja's father, was of course one of the first to bring home a 'Loewe Opta' television set. Besides that, nothing was new about neighbourhood kids joining the family to watch a TV program. When, during the show of that day, monkeys played their role in the African jungle, Arja thought it would be funny to call out to Kulervo, "Look, this is you playing in the jungle and going after your friends." This was too much for Kulervo who stood up and left without a word, failing from then on to come and see Arja anymore.

Forty years later during a Finland visit with her husband, Arja and Martin paid a visit in the neighbourhood to Kulervo and his family. What had upset him when we were young, now, forty years later, became a matter of laughter for everyone. All was well that ended well. His family welcomed Arja and her husband so heartily that they could only respond with the warmest welcome for them to visit them in Australia. They considered this highly unlikely simply because of the distance between Australia and Finland. A meeting in later life highlighted was the idea that during life we all change, and therefore often look back on previous events from a safe distance in our minds.

The end of another summer holiday was quickly followed by another year at school. In Arja's case, this meant repeating the previous year and making sure she left behind last year's poor performance. She needed to move forward strongly for the final year's examinations. Somehow, Arja had changed during these last summer school holidays and went back to the school in Nokia with a clear, fresh mind. The year 1964 presented her with realities. Nobody asked whether or not she liked them; they simply summed up life at that time.

One of these incidents was the illness of Arja's grandpa in Pispala, a suburb of Tampere, where she had lived during the time at school in Nokia. Artturi, her grandpa, had only two years earlier survived a ruptured appendix. He was now in his late seventies and he never really recovered. His kindness towards a younger generation - keeping a close eye on Arja and trusting everybody in the family with honesty and readiness to help - brought her very close to both her grandparents. Never grumbling, they understood the younger generation's urgencies by playing down a disagreement with, "Time eventually will tell who of us is right; tomorrow will be another day and the sun might shine again on all of us. Nothing has ever been that urgent that it couldn't wait another day."

Artturi must have known by then that his time was up, as he wished already in his frail condition to die in his bed and not in the hospital. Over a number of months, Arja sat at night next to his bed reading out of a book, which she knew he had read many times over during his life. The bookshelf in the living room didn't show a great number of different-sized volumes. However, all books were always placed in an orderly fashion in the same spot as long as Arja could remember back. While reading, she also prepared slices of an apple by peeling off the skin with a knife's edge. This took Artturi all the time to eat bit by bit.

One night Arja had planned to visit a play in the local open-air theatre together with her aunt Aune. When telling her grandpa about it, his words came out slowly as if they came from far away, "You better go to the theatre; I'll be all right. The winter ice on our lakes hasn't yet retreated entirely. I will go with the ice." Returning home late at night from the theatre, Arja's grandmum was not waiting as usual in the living room. Usually she was reading something by herself after a long day's work, but this night Arja knew that something wasn't right and she recalls the sadness of that night.

"*Not long after I arrived home, grandma emerged silently from grandpa's bedroom, dressed in a black costume and placing her fingers to her lips, "Psst, Arja come and say your goodbyes to Artturi." Only a dim light near the bed was on, grandpa lay in bed so silent so peaceful, I could not hold back the tears in my eyes. His face reflected rest while his closed eyes had retreated from life's vision; not one single wrinkle crossed the smooth surface of his skin. Grandma stood in silence next to me putting her arm on my shoulder while holding my hand with the other one, finally breaking her silence with slow, calm words, "You better go to bed and seek some rest from the long day." Together we left the bedroom for the brighter lightened living room. I felt so helplessly empty as this was the first time in my young life I had experienced the loss of a loved one. During that night, I couldn't sleep at all, memories turned up incessantly like a silent film behind my closed eyes.*

"*The following morning I couldn't get ready for school in time, despite a written test waiting at school for me. Grand mum only sympathized with me; the day at school was called off. Still in the early morning hours, black dressed men came into the house, taking grandpa on stretchers into a black van, which waited in front of the house. These moments appeared to me like a second farewell before the last one at the cemetery. I couldn't help, but to think by myself, why is it that we have to leave this life, a life we cherish so much perhaps even if it was less fortunate. Where are the answers to it? Isn't life a gift equally important even after it has ceased to be?*"

This was the message bringing everybody to the funeral, close family and so many customers of the grocery shop over so many years. All wanted to acknowledge that life will continue. Almost the whole community of the country suburb of Pispala turned up, paying their respect to one of their citizens - not a famous citizen, but one who has earned the respect of everybody over a period of a whole lifetime without having made one enemy. The changed conditions at number 59 Pispalanvaltatie (Pispalan-Road), called for reduced activities in the shop on the ground floor. First, the ice delivery in the early hours of every day was suspended together with the delivery of the milk in cans. Arja's grandma and aunt couldn't run the whole business any more. They planned to cut back services gradually, letting locals know about it over time so that the family could retire in more privacy upstairs in the house.

    At the rate Arja's life developed, especially during 1964, everything seemed to happen - not just less fortunate things but the more positive, overall success at the school in Nokia. This happened because of changes, which affected views towards her own life. Since having moved away from her hometown, new people and new conditions challenged what Arja had experienced under the protection of a well-guided home run mainly by her mother. She had to start thinking more for herself as her mum made the decision to separate from Arja's father in order to lead a more predictable life in the future. The lifestyle of Petteri had caused Tysse too many sleepless nights, which she was determined to leave behind once and for all as her two daughters grew into adulthood supported by her continuous assistance.

    The time had then arrived that she also looked after her well-being before reaching a point of irreversible damage to her own health. The cost was that she had to look for work to support her own needs. No separation of a husband and wife happens without pain. In the process, Arja's younger sister became more uncertain as to which side to support. Eventually, she decided to stick with her mum while at least keeping the road open to dad, because something beneficial still might come from both sides. This was not Arja's focus. Quietly, she opted to stay with her mum, showing her support even if there was only very little that she could do. Arja's best shot undoubtedly became to finish the school year as second best in the class.

Still in 1964, after her mum and dad had separated, Arja's mum also took the step of selling the home at Honkaistenranta, outside Turku. The house and the property became too much of a load for Tysse since Arja lived during school time in Tampere with her grand mum and aunt as her mum had taken on work in town. Therefore, her moving into a city apartment in 'Satakunantie' made perfect sense with regard to the family's changed conditions. Arja was under the best possible care of her grandmother, which wasn't the case so much with her sister. She remained first with her mum, but since her mum pursued work, time developed into a sparse commodity compared with previous years.

This change in the family life possibly supported also the different directions Arja and her sister took in their lives. Arja remained at school, pursuing her first goal of finishing school to the best of her ability so that she could continue with a higher education. With the end of the school year at the end of May 1965, the teachers had given Arja all the good marks she could have wished for. Since returning from England, her life at school had made a change for the better and the personal confidence gained out of it, helped her to enjoy school, at least towards the end when school essentially determined her future life.

Arja's first decision for the summer school holidays was to see her mum in Turku and to see for herself how Thysse was managing her role in a new life. Arja's Mum would never have complained; she was the same as before, receiving Arja with joyfulness and happiness. As a grown up daughter, she couldn't miss however that there was more than the eye possibly could see. In a sense, her mum really didn't deserve the daily struggle for her own life, including that of her two daughters.

Only when time had passed, did she sometimes reveal her life with Arja's dad. Not all was bad, of course, but the downsides of Petteri's extravagant life didn't fit the background her mum came from. It was a very humble, diligent working family with a strong sense of decent tradition shared in a practical, Finnish Protestant attitude. Arja had experienced all this with her grandparents for which she's been grateful all her life. The personal freedom out of such a life inspired Arja early on to keep away from people with uncertain attitudes. In fact, she remained wary especially towards approaches from the other gender. The faith of her mother gave Arja reason enough to stay at a distance, instead of becoming too closely involved in friendly relations.

The irresolution in Arja's family could on one hand be regarded in today's terms as an unfortunate case. But on the other hand Arja had no reason to feel let down by her own family, because her mother had early enough put in place measures to safeguard. She could do this with the help of her own parents resulting in a less disrupted future for Arja and her sister. A mother like that is the greatest gift one can have in a life.

After a week or so in Turku at the beginning of the 1965 summer holidays, Arja and her mum had to do a lot of catching up because of all the months Arja had been away living with her grandma. Her experience in England the previous year fostered a plan to go abroad again, at least for a few weeks. The family's changed living conditions didn't allow her mum to support her financially anymore as on the trip to England. Petteri had not completely moved out of their lives, occasionally turning up to help Thysse when life turned a bit towards the tougher side. Arja's good school results inspired him to give her a helping hand so that she could make the boat trip across to neighbouring Stockholm, in Sweden, where, through prior correspondence, she had organized work in a hospital. Arja's Mum fully supported her plan, as she believed that young people should go out and learn for themselves from conditions other than the accustomed ones at home. A good home is there to firstly establish a solid foundation from which a young life can move into more directions for their own benefit. Such foundation emerges sound only when put to the test outside familiar daily boundaries.

CHAPTER 6

Away From Finland: Meeting Martin

Arja's second passage across the Baltic Sea to Sweden went almost like clockwork. In summer, during holidays, the ships connecting Finland and Sweden were mostly fully booked out. The passage was quite affordable if one travelled on the ship's tourist decks. It was possible to occupy one of the many seats under closed decks with window views to the outside.

Before leaving Turku by ship, Arja paid her best friend Tuija a visit. Tuija had left school at 'middle level', now working every day of the week in a transport company. Therefore, it was only the weekend that was available to meet. Tuija's dad had also caused her family lots of uncertain times. Tuija's mother, like Arja's mother, came from very decent family stock, so that both families had found common ground in supporting each other. The main difference between the two fathers was that Arja's dad had never been caught in 'flagrante delicto', thereby sparing his family the upheavals resulting out of such a circumstance.

Arja's mum always lent Tuija's family a helping hand to get through the worst of these incidents. Difficulties only brought the two families closer together. Arja considered herself privileged to be able to stay at school, whereas her friend Tuija had to begin work at an earlier stage of her life. This didn't change Tuija however; she still maintained her joyful nature. Each time the girls met, especially after longer periods of time, there was always a lot of catching up to do, recounting what had taken place in their lives since the last visit. They never really lost contact even throughout Arja's longer absences from Finland later on. It proved to be true that absence can make the heart grow fonder.

Working during her holidays also gave Arja a sense of 'real' life outside school. The support from her mother and, in this case, also from father Petteri gave her the start to go to Sweden. Working conditions in Sweden were at that time better than in Finland so that Arja could save money to lighten the burden on her mum when she returned to Finland.

After a glorious passage through the archipelago, which lies widespread before Finland, the ship arrived in Stockholm, unloading its large number of passengers as if an invasion into Sweden had started. Surprisingly, everybody dispersed in a very short time. A large amount of young people were holidaying in Sweden, travelling further south from here to neighbouring Denmark and Germany. Some, like Arja, were seeking employment to earn money for their own lives. Arja had her job lined up in a hospital from Finland so that she had an address to go to straight after her arrival.

Stockholm has always been a city with open spaces, because of the sea-arms dividing its many modern housing estates from each other. Arja's time in Stockholm from mid June until the end of July passed very quickly, leaving very little time for planning anything else outside working hours of the hospital. As Arja received accommodation within the hospital zone, she kept to this area in order to give her hard-earned money a better chance of accumulating. It didn't escape Arja's attention that men as well as women appeared, in certain cases, obtrusive with their sexual advances. At the time, Finland and Sweden were very different in that regard.

Here in Sweden, personal freedom found more expressions in the name of progress than Arja was prepared to admit to herself. She had been raised to believe that individual ideals shouldn't be guided by a dominant trend of public life. Shouldn't we safeguard our personal feelings and change them only with caution throughout life? In matters of sympathy for somebody else, we determine where we stand. Arja saw plenty of free expressions of love around her, giving her something to think about while she was away from parental guidance. Somewhere down the line during life, everybody will find himself at a crossroad where it is necessary to make an individual decision about which direction to take.

For such a reason, it is useful to break out of a guided life from time to time in order to find one's own ground to stand on in new challenges. Nothing can stand on its own if it has not been challenged. Modeling and guidance from one's own family, school and friends play a vital role in life's decisions. It always remains important not to rush anything in life; rather, give it time in order to gain a better insight into the so many hidden agendas surrounding our lives.

Arja's last day in the Stockholm hospital had arrived and it was time to think about her return to Finland. The work with patients, keeping the assigned ward clean and in order, and working jointly with the permanent staff, filled her working days. The money saved during her stay also gave Arja some satisfaction. The hospital allowed her to stay for a couple of days longer in their accommodation so that she could organize her return trip to Finland and also have a bit of time for sightseeing, mainly in Stockholm.

The majority of people here were friendly and forthcoming, especially when conversations were held in Swedish. It was up to Arja to make herself understood. Again, she had to move beyond her school knowledge of Swedish in order to satisfy the work interactions with others. Occasional passing shots about her Finnish-Swedish tongue, including the rhythm and cadence, didn't bother Arja too much. At least she didn't show it, maintaining the 'underdog' role by listening rather than trying to make a point, which would certainly be inappropriate, considering that she was a visitor from another country.

Straight after her work at the hospital had ended, Arja went to the travel agency at the docking place where the ships anchored for Finland. It was a real 'Sun' day, exceptionally warm with a cloudless blue sky. The following day, Monday, a ship was destined for Turku; there was one booking left open. With the ticket in her hand, Arja had the rest of the day at her disposal. Nothing seemed more natural, in view of the brilliant weather, than to stroll along the embankment in front of the imposing King Palaces.

Hardly anybody else was on foot within a fair distance from the main traffic arterials. These main roads joined other road intersections in both directions. They were free standing on pillars rising off the ground. Arja remembers another pedestrian, however, who came across her path, asking her in English about the time of the day.

Memories going back

"Normally I would have been puzzled as to why somebody asked me such a question, but history proved, the same young man happened also to ask me two years later to become his wife, which I then happily agreed on. Now, I realized from the gentleman's English accent that he also was not a local. After telling him the time, I don't know why I engaged in a conversation, which was out of place with my usual practice.

"Would you like to listen to guitar music?" the gentleman asked me.

"I like guitar-music, but I can't see where the music would come from," I responded. It was in a sense unusual, because I was the last person who would talk to a stranger. 'Guitar music' however proved me wrong.

"I have my guitar in the youth hostel not far from here. Would you like to wait here until I return with my guitar?"

In fact, I did wait, watching the young man running the distance until disappearing from my sight. As I started to question why I was waiting for a stranger, the same man appeared with a guitar case, rushing towards me. On arrival, out of breath, he started a conversation suggesting that we both walk across the next bridge to the opposite shore where a picturesque sailing ship anchored alongside slopes of green grass. Was I fascinated or caught by something, I couldn't say at that moment. Perhaps both of us experienced something like this. In fact, we both went on foot across a pedestrian bridge with a golden crown on its railing. In the sailing ship's shade, on a perfect green lawn, we sat opposite each other for the next hour or so, not much concerned about the time of the day any more as I enjoyed being entertained by the gentleman on the guitar, who also sang to the guitar.

"You performed very well with your guitar. Thank you very much; I enjoyed it. I should return to the ship now."

"Would you like me to accompany you?"

"If you don't mind."

"Not much talking went on while we walked back the way we came. In close proximity to the first ship on the quay, I mentioned for the first time that I came from Turku in Finland and was about to return home by ship. The gentleman appeared at a loss about Finnish geography, reassuring me that he would have a good look next time he got a map in front of him. Despite this, when exchanging our first names,

I was convinced I would not remember the gentleman's name for long. However, he produced his visiting card, asking me to accept it and keep it, in order to write to him from Finland. I thought, well, here I have another penfriend, this time one from Germany. When 'brevity is the soul of wit', it worked in our case!

"*The following day when the ship was due to leave, the weather had turned around so miserably that I began longing for the beautiful conditions of yesterday. Secretly, I did hope to see this Martin come to the ship and say farewell to me. This however didn't happen. The cold and the heavy rain of the day had put on hold this sort of a wish. I had to admit not only to having enjoyed the guitar concert, but especially the originality of this meeting during which Martin displayed a courtesy I could not forget. His smile too did not escape my attention, while I really couldn't figure out what pleased him about me during our short meeting. Did I also have such a smile on my face? Time slowly answered 'yes', because there had been at least a hidden spark of affection on either side, smouldering steadily along until turning into the fire of a life-long relationship.*

"*Not long after having returned to Finland, I kept my promise and wrote a few sentences in English to Martin's address in Germany. "You might remember me from Stockholm? I thank you very much again for your guitar concert, which in my memory I shall cherish very much. If you like, please also write to me at my address attached to my letter. In Finnish we say 'terveisin', (see you again), Arja."*

"*What once more became important was to resume daily routines before heading to Tampere in order to attend the last year of school in Nokia. This was crucial for any future planning; no matter what direction I should take. I spent almost a fortnight with mum in the new flat, realizing with the tighter living conditions, that life was not the same anymore. In previous years, we had owned a spacious house and garden. Mum never complained about this new situation we all found ourselves in, remaining instead the same joyful, and caring mother.*"

Adjusting to work life in a shopping centre demanded some personal sacrifices for her, which she took on supported by the knowledge that her two daughters had reached a stage in their lives from where they could continue more independently. Arja's life with her grand mum and her mother's younger sister in Tampere provided her still with undiminished family support. Her younger sister, despite living closer to her mum, had much earlier chosen to lead her own life. Arja's sister was not one to enjoy school and learn from there. In that regard, the sisters were differently gifted. In everything they did, Arja's sister was the quick one as well as being highly skilled. Arja felt that this was very different from her.

However, her mum used to say, "You are a good daughter too, Arja. Slow and steady will also get you somewhere in life. Your dad leads life in the fast lane. I am so glad that you are not the same way. Stay as you are and achieve something in life for yourself. You know you have my unconditional support. I am so proud of you. Don't worry too much about my life. You have everything in front of you and have all the reason in the world to look forward to a good future. Knowing that you will not forget me gives me the strength daily to continue together with the whole of my family."

Arja couldn't think of a better affirmation from a mother. Before taking the train again to Tampere to honour the trust she had received from those at 'home', Arja thought about Martin. Her mum hadn't yet received knowledge of their surprise meeting in Stockholm. An advertising sign about a guitar concert in the university theatre gave Arja the opportunity to tell her mum about her experience in Stockholm, inviting her at the same time to this concert. Proudly, she also paid for her mother's ticket out of her own savings. In the past, her mum had paid for lessons on the piano, at which Arja hadn't progressed with overwhelming enthusiasm.

Her sudden interest for guitar music visibly surprised her mum when Arja told her about her personal guitar concert in Stockholm. "Arja, Arja, who was the better, the music or the musician?" After their joint concert visit on the university premises, Arja's mum in her excitement confirmed the pleasure she experienced in the guitar performance. Guitar music is a voice from countries far away from Finland telling of the joy, pain, and hope all people experience in life, in which individual imagination can make people travel into a fabulous distant world.

Such introduction prepared Arja's mum for a letter from her daughter's guitar player from Stockholm. Her mum could only shake her head on hearing that Arja was going to receive another letter from Germany. "How many penpals have you got by now? It must be close to forty." Martin might become number forty-one, if he was to answer Arja's letter which she dearly hoped he would because his introduction was romantic and in style.

"Since your return, I have realized that you carried some secret joy around with you. Is my Arja experiencing first love?"

"No mum. I am not stupid, you know me."

"Well, we have all said this and when it comes, nothing can stop it anymore."

"I am only looking forward to a new penpal, who told me already that he has seen other countries. This makes him different from all the others. He is, by the way, also a student from the University of Heidelberg and had most interesting antecedents before going to study, which I only briefly heard him mention in Stockholm."

The realities of daily life meanwhile took over from holiday time, forcing the new experiences to retreat, but not driving them completely out of Arja's mind. Back in Tampere with her grand mum and again attending school regularly in Nokia, the routine, which had changed during school holidays, had to be regained. Arja had been a serious student last school year and she needed to be so again. Her turnaround into success in the previous class had to be maintained if she wanted to carry on with a higher education after school. At the age of twenty, Arja was not experienced enough to fully understand for herself the need or benefit of a further education. It was only during the years that followed that Arja concluded that all that was useful in life came not just from school learning. Life has always been the best teacher and one can learn a lot if standing with one leg in each camp – study and the reality of daily life.

Meanwhile the letter from Germany to her address in Turku found its way to Tampere thanks to her mum redirecting it. School required undiminished attention at that decisive last stage so that Arja spent much less time on correspondence with penfriends. Most of them stopped writing altogether at that time, whereas her guitar player continued writing letters at great length.

The end of 1965 drew closer in no time at all because it was packed with so much to do. The one particular penfriend from Germany must had started wondering why Arja was not writing anymore and as a consequence announced a visit to find out the answer for himself. The winter of 1965/66 happened to be one of the coldest in recent Finnish history. Therefore, it seemed highly unlikely that somebody would have made the journey through snow and the frozen Baltic Sea to Finland at that time. During the Christmas school break, Arja went to see her mum again in the flat in Turku. When telling her about the guitar-playing romantic wanting to visit her during the first days in January, her mum couldn't help laughing, "Here you are. He can't come just like that. We might have to wait and see whether or not our current winter, with temperatures exceeding minus forty degree Celsius, will allow him to make this journey."

Arja hesitated, but simply started the waiting game. Because of the severe winter conditions, Christmas was celebrated at the home in Turku. On Christmas Eve, it was tradition to first visit the cemetery and light a candle in a bowl at the graveside of a family member. As the descendents of Arja's mother came from Tampere, the family paid their respect every year in that place. This year, however, the weather only allowed for travel by train towards the last days of the year, so it was past New Year when the family met in Tampere.

Arja only then remembered that a visitor might arrive very shortly in Turku. When asking her mum what to do, she responded, "Do you really think somebody is coming to see us during this time of the year? Well, what we could do to cover all eventualities is to return to Turku on the weekend. That should be good enough; our visitor won't come to Finland for only one day."

And that was that. However, when returning to Turku, a surprise awaited. A magnificent bouquet of red carnations hung on the knob of the family's front door. Attached was a card:'With compliments from Martin'. Arja's mum was the first to be delighted, taking the flowers off the door and putting them in a vase.

"Where might this gentleman be now?" Even her mum became curious to see Arja's latest penfriend. "He appears to be a real gentleman." Nothing could be done other than waiting and so they carried on with the day's program. The following morning when the phone rang, her mum ordered Arja to take the call in case it was the 'flower man'. And indeed, it was him, calling from a hotel in the city. Arja didn't hesitate to invite him to come and visit the family, not forgetting to thank him for his pleasant introduction of the red carnations.

Arja remembers speaking on the phone in English and how nervous her mum was, asking hurriedly, "What did he say; is he really coming?"

"Nobody could have said for sure, who was more excited, mum or me. The bell at the door sounded not much more than an hour after our telephone conversation.

"A tall gentleman dressed in winter gear stood with a smile on his face and opening with a comment in Finnish, "Hyyvaa paiva, minun niemi on Martin (Good day, my name is Martin)." That was about how far his Finnish carried him during the excitement. Not much else had to be said however as I stood next to the door, indicating with my hand to come in. All the while, I received encouragement from my mother behind me. The first moments, always likely to be the most difficult ones, passed better than the three of us could probably have expected. My mother pointed to the red carnations in a vase on the table and no words were needed; the flowers said it all.

"A slowly developing conversation moved backwards and forwards between us in English and Finnish. The initial anxiety eased by the minute and everybody experienced a most friendly welcome. Nobody had to feel like a stranger at all. In a joint effort, a plan was quickly made as how to make the most out of a short visit

for our guest. Moving one step at a time allowed everybody to become familiar with this unique situation.

"*It didn't take much time to show the small flat to our very polite guest, Martin. The views from the higher level of our flat into the outside winter scenery offered the best attraction for the moment. It was especially beautiful, looking from the comfort of a well-heated atmosphere out onto a white snowy layer, which crossed the whole country. On the road that passed in the distance, cars and buses followed tyre trails in the snow at almost normal speed. Besides other houses around the area, only the dark green of the forest glittered through the white snow 'cushions', while a dark grey sky promised more snow to come. By reflecting sparse daylight mainly from the white snowfields, this was often the only bright point of the day.*

"Show your guest around town after we have a good, hot cup of coffee and something to eat," mum suggested, continuing also, "Today it is fortunately not as cold as it has been over the past couple of days."

"*A bus not far from our address serviced the community with a regular run into and out of the city. Many drivers store their cars away during winter as it becomes very difficult to run a car when cold, snow and ice have their firm grip across this northern part of Europe. Stepping out of the house usually tells you straight away, what the real weather conditions are. When wind joins the other elements, it makes the cold feel twice as bad. Snow is everywhere, not even stopping when passengers enter the bus. It is only when the entrance door was shut that the snow was locked out. Puddles of melting snow on the bus floor created a messy picture, not doing much to keep the cold outside or to stop it from moving through the bus, as if these conditions were normal. However, the bus caught my attention especially when starting on the snow surface. Instead of starting slowly as one would have thought, the bus revved its wheels until slowly picking up speed, which must be the way to drive on slippery surfaces.*

The city centre of Turku consisted of a big square centre surrounded by major buildings such as the only Orthodox Church in the place or the shopping centre 'Wiklund' where mum worked during the week. The weather wasn't much good for outdoor sightseeing, suggesting rather indoor visits to the museum in the castle and parts of the University complex. Turku also has a history of a connection to the

'Hanse-Towns' (Seaport Cities) from around the Baltic Sea. These start in the neighbourhood of Tallinn, Riga, and further south leading to Kaliningrad, Gdansk, Rostock, Lubeck, and Kiel. This is also reflected in local museum exhibits. By showing my guest Martin, the University, I wanted to give him an understanding of what the Uni here looks like. Hopefully during summer of this year, it would be the place I wanted to continue at after school.

"You have a small, very nice facility here for studies, not as big and overcrowded as Heidelberg." Thus were the comments of my guest. Nobody else besides us was visiting the museum or the University at this time. The winter, New Year holiday created a quiet atmosphere. During these visits, I also made the point that I felt honoured to have received a visit from a penfriend but made myself clear that in order to remain good friends; we don't have to share everything.

"I am probably different from so many others. Normally I would not spend my time with men. You are already an exemption; please respect it."

The point was made and that was that. Later in the afternoon, a cinema visit alternated with the time we had walked during the day. James Bond's 'Thunderbird' was screening in a local cinema. The well-heated theatre and comfortable seats indeed invited quite a number of people to view this spectacle. Just before the start of the show, my sister turned up, joined by other friends, taking their seats right behind us. This didn't happen by pure accident. More likely it was out of curiosity. After I had introduced her briefly, my sister emphasized her actions with a comment to us both, "Surprise, surprise, my sister Arja who never wants to get married, has a boyfriend now. Somebody has to keep an eye on you both."

The show over, my first meeting with my penfriend from another country ended soon after. Martin had booked his return passage for the next morning. Time to say 'nakemiin' (good-bye) after the cinema, with a formal handshake and the farewell wish to keep in touch. Speaking for myself, a special visit was over. Life had to continue in very predictable ways for me so close to matriculation. Priorities demanded a break in my correspondence during which everybody except one stopped writing altogether. The one continuing to write, despite very little response from my side, was of course Martin. Why he did so, amused me at the time on several occasions."

Meanwhile the winter didn't cease with its severe cold throughout the month of February. This was also the month during which the last school year officially ended. Preparation time and exams followed over the next ten weeks. Before this scrutiny started, a custom amongst schools was to celebrate the farewell to school years. In a way, it could have been called an early celebration, as none of the students really could know whether he/she would pass the examinations that lay ahead. That early celebration was at least not wasted, regardless of the examination outcome. Students used to take to the streets on anything driveable that they could possibly put their hands, whether it was a tractor, a veteran car, or motorbike.

This year, however, winter diminished a lot of the fun of the event from the start. The temperature was crazy, dropping during the day to around minus thirty degrees Celsius. Fanned by gusty winds, it became even less tolerable. As a consequence, none of the public turned up to watch our 'circus display' as it moved through the town of Nokia. All the candidates of Arja's class, twenty in all, were kept busy trying to keep the cold under control. Despite the odds against them, it can be said beforehand that all made it through the farewell drive-party and, with only a few exemptions, most passed the exams later on. The cold couldn't harm the way of an inauguration.

Most importantly also Arja passed the examinations 'cum laude'. On hearing about her school finals, father Petteri couldn't help but join the family and present Arja with a voucher for car driving lessons after having returned to her hometown of Turku. Petteri showed as much pride as if he had achieved the school final results himself. No harm was done to anybody in the family by occasionally revisiting the family 'harbour' except for Arja's mum, who refused to re-enter into a relationship with Petteri. The past with him had hurt her personal pride too many times, beyond a possible return to normality in trust. This didn't stop Petteri repeatedly asking for forgiveness.

Last school year, Arja-Nokia/Finland

Yet Arja's mum knew too well that this husband couldn't keep his word. After playing his role of the good husband convincingly, each time was shorter and shorter. From a distance, Arja could see past all this, recognizing the strong, colourful personality of her dad in a more positive light, which didn't however miss the mark of the shady sides of his life. Such views moulded Arja on the one hand into a person with an open mind, but on the other hand, she could be very critical. This was because she had experienced firsthand in her family how people can live with different personas like those that her dad did.

Arja's sympathy for her mother was certainly explained by their close affiliation to each other. It also explained Arja's habit of keeping a cautious distance from newcomers. This was the guiding way of a young person who was growing into adulthood. The official age to be declared an adult at that time was twenty-one years. This could be regarded only as a target, as life especially can teach us later on that we never stop learning as long as we live. Looking from there, when do we really reach adulthood in its true sense within a lifespan? Apart from that, life has always continued regardless of the views we develop, and so did Arja's.

CHAPTER 7

Enrolment in Finland: Heidelberg/Germany

With school life left behind, Arja suddenly felt as free as a bird whose wings could carry it to new horizons. The summer of 1967 lay ahead and an unforeseen present came from her aunt in Tampere. "For your school finals, I'd like you to receive a reward from me as you have reached your goal in a life lived closely with grand mum and myself. What would you like to do with a little money from us?"

Arja's answer was as straightforward as if she had thought about it beforehand. "I want to travel again and if possible, return the courtesy visit of Martin."

"Oh, I see you haven't forgotten your guitar player!" Arja's plan to travel to Heidelberg was given the thumbs up by her mum. Euphoria had set into Arja's life. As Martin studied medicine in Heidelberg, Arja wanted to reach out to him and enroll in medicine at Turku University. Alas, it wasn't to be, because, during the preparation semester at Turku University, Arja learned that her science knowledge from school left her high and dry during the tests. Arja simply was not prepared for so much math, physics and chemistry, which were not her strongest interests anyway.

In order not to lose undue time, enrolment into theology at the Uni seemed better for her. Having then decided on a new direction, the time after the summer break became a good opportunity to prepare for her travel plans, endowed with all possible recommendations from all sides of the family and of course, their subsequent good wishes.

In the middle of July in 1966, the train took Arja on the first leg of her trip to Helsinki. The train was necessary because ships going across the Baltic Sea then south to Lubeck in Germany only departed from Finland's capital. The big modern ship steamed with its full load of passengers, plus a fully loaded lower deck of vehicles, trucks and buses, taking less than two days amidst brilliant sunshine to cross a calm Baltic Sea.

To Arja's surprise, her penpal Martin welcomed her on the ship's arrival in Lubeck. He had chosen to hitchhike from Heidelberg to Lubeck and asked Arja whether she would join him on the way south to Heidelberg. Arja did not reveal that she had a train ticket for this leg of the journey. This new way of travelling caught her interest. Together Martin and Arja tried in vain for an hour or two to get a lift with one of the passengers, who continued their journey by car. When unsuccessful, they changed their plan into two different ones. One person can get a lift much easier than two can, so Martin would continue to seek a lift. As Arja had a train ticket, she would go by train to Heidelberg. Martin gave her his address and also the one of his friend Harro in case Arja arrived earlier than he did. Martin looked forward to meeting Arja again in Heidelberg as soon as possible. He knew his friend meanwhile would take care of her.

They parted with Martin saying, "I am so happy to see you again. You are a beautiful penpal."

To be honest, the welcome was definitely unconventional, but Arja realized that student life had its own rules driven by different decisions from most other people's lives. To find a solution to any problem appeared an action of very personal courage to which she felt herself drawn. The reason for that might have been the fact that she had grown up perfectly protected from the outside world, gaining only a small window of insight through her hobby of reading.

This meeting with her penpal Martin in Stockholm, then in Turku and now on German soil became for Arja like a continuing story in one of her books. It looked to her like her own creation, something not known to her before. All was new territory and most of all encouraging, since indeed she had learned that there are people actually doing things instead of just starting a talkfest.

In fact, Martin arrived in Heidelberg on the same day Arja arrived by train. His friend Harro, also a student and subtenant of an elderly, single, pensioner lady, welcomed Arja and introduced her to his landlord. It was as if this was the most natural occurrence in the world: somebody arriving in Germany from Finland and conversing first in English and then not long after, for the first time having a conversation in German with the house lady, as she couldn't speak any English. Arja surprised herself with how freely she responded to a completely new situation in a new environment.

Returning kindness becomes so easy when it is first offered to you and it was not only the kind of polite phrase, but also one could feel that it came from the bottom of the heart. Was this because the landlady was at an advanced age looking at life from a distant experience? It certainly was the case when she expressed her concern about Arja's stay in Heidelberg.

"Ladies, whether students, married or not, do not stay in my house overnight. I hope you have made arrangements for your Finland visitor somewhere else."

Everybody present was astonished when Arja confirmed that before arriving she had organized her own accommodation in a nearby restaurant called 'Zum Gruenen Laub' (At the Green Foliage). After all that travelling, it was good to call it a day. The landlady was left to her own devices while Arja received company on the way to her accommodation.

"How could you possibly organize this nice place to stay in Heidelberg so quickly?" Martin asked, adding, "You are quite clever at organizing yourself."

Anxiously listening to this compliment, Arja responded, "If wanting something bad enough, one will eventually succeed. I am just learning and in a foreign country, there is much more to learn. Thank you for accompanying me to the restaurant. I need a good night's sleep badly. Tomorrow will be another day to which I am looking forward already. Sleep well."

"What time would you like me to come around and pick you up? Is nine o'clock all right with you?"

"Yes of course! You don't know how happy I am to see you again."

"What about you Arja?"

"I won't take you into the restaurant, but I do still appreciate our friendship. Please respect it. So far, you have made such a good impression; please keep it that way. Goodnight and see you again tomorrow."

The next day, the weather turned out to be a mixed bag of everything but definitely not summer. The temperature barely reached ten degrees and rain out of a closed grey sky made the couple rethink the plan of sightseeing in and around Heidelberg. After a good night's sleep, Arja was ready again to tackle a new day regardless of the weather and agreed to use the day for a plan which Martin had in mind. "Let's go instead to Frankfurt for the day, where I have to respond to an employment opportunity with Boeing in America. The current Vietnam War doesn't encourage me to go to America despite the excellent conditions I am offered. Arja, would you be prepared to come to America with me?"

Arja had no quick answer to this, but found out on this occasion that Martin had also a previous education as an engineer, working regularly during university breaks to earn money for his living and studies. When Arja couldn't say anything, Martin briefly said, "If you don't go, I am not going either. So let's go together to Frankfurt to cancel my appointment with Boeing."

The weather remained miserable for the whole day. They were pleased they were not looking at Heidelberg on such a cold and overcast day. On the train and during their stay in Frankfurt, Martin mentioned that he lived on his own, not having a very good relationship with his stepparents. He used this excuse for not being able to welcome her by introducing his family as he had experienced in Finland.

"The poor thing must be used to battling all his life," Arja thought to herself.

Frankfurt took most of the day to explore. During this time, nothing was boring, especially because Martin knew to tell many interesting stories, so different from the life Arja had experienced in her guarded family environment. Hailing from old traditional farmer stock of Transylvania in Romania, Martin not only lost his family during World War II, but also ended up a stolen refugee in Germany. Ever since, he had been on the move more than would probably have been ideal.

Arja couldn't help feeling sorry when learning about other people's lives, but she also recognized how good her own life was. What impressed her most was the positive attitude of Martin, never falling short of kindness nor complaining about anything. Arja thought she had learnt something so far in her life only to realize then, there was much more to learn from other people.

One miserable day's weather is usually followed by sunshine the next day. Heidelberg showed its bright side the next day within its location at the end of a valley between steeply rising hill sites, densely forested by deciduous trees. This was not at all like the dark green pine forests of Finland. An historical castle overlooks the old city centre from a ridge as it creeps along the river squeezed between the hill sites. It houses the biggest historical wine barrel in the world. On a sunny day, views from there spread out over the plain, which leads out to the river Rhine.

A few old stone bridges span across the river Neckar, connecting both shores. This causes dense traffic situations in the city as centuries ago cobbled streets were not built for today's traffic. Narrow alleys run along between centuries old buildings, all massively constructed in local sandstone with many of their facades ornamentally presented. There were also different University departments spread around the city, which Martin showed Arja as they travelled on foot through the city centre. Later additions to the University were found outside the historical city centre, which meant a lot of moving around for students at that time.

A long day of sightseeing undoubtedly makes feet tired, and a rest on a seat at Martin's friend place was a welcome change. Harro had his fiancée, who came from Scotland, living with him. An improvised student lunch where everybody contributed something, was the beginning of an evening of conversation, guitar music and singing. The atmosphere was great because everybody took part in one way or another, contributing something from their own personal background. Someone had news from Scotland while Arja shared something from Finland. It was evident that the person who travels can see and tell a lot.

Arja retained a bit of her 'Finnish timidity', not being entirely confident in such a new environment outside her own country. She liked music too, but when it came to practicing it, she was a long way behind the other three who performed by singing and playing the guitar. Luckily, she was not asked to perform. Instead, Martin did the honours and it was understood that not everybody is good at everything. For Arja, the main thing remained to gain a window into a world she previously hadn't experienced.

The group entertained themselves without the need of somebody else doing it. Martin and his close friend Harro looked back to the same background of the Boy Scout movement, which in those days fostered a culture of self-activities comprising almost all areas of daily life: creativity, education, discipline, help, physical exercise, nature awareness, and societal integration. All this over many years during childhood following well into adulthood had marked a lasting personal independence.

There was one day left on Arja's planned stay in Heidelberg. In order not to spoil this day with a late start, the night before was ended at a reasonable hour. Besides, the co-inhabitants of the house in which they had gathered, reminded them with blows to the wall that it was time for night peace. This was something Arja never became aware of in Finland, probably because the people she knew, including her own family, mostly lived in their own houses. It was only when her mother moved into a city flat in a tall city building with many other co- inhabitants that she became barred by the neighbours from playing the piano. Obviously, where people live closer together, more rules are necessary.

The last day on the Heidelberg trip turned into a hot summer's day, ideal to take to the water, which the little group did. On the river Neckar, all four set a folding boat afloat, which Martin and Harro had taken all the way down the river Rhone from Switzerland to the Mediterranean two years earlier. The difference this time however was that from the start this time four people boarded the boat, which previously carried only two. Testing the boat on the side of the river for stability with its load of four went without a hiccup.

Not long after floating downstream with the river towards its centre, for no known reason, the boat suddenly tipped over to one side sending everybody into the water for a swim. Everybody burst into laughter except one, Harro's fiancée. She disappeared like a stone on to the riverbed obviously not trying to move away from there. Harro, a very good swimmer, instantly dived down pulling her up to the surface. He was also the only one to know that his fiancée couldn't swim at all. The incident turned a bit unpleasant since the rescued girl accused everybody of negligence.

Arja did her best to calm down the Scottish passenger without much success. The day was from then on slightly spoiled. The two parties separated and at least Martin and Arja didn't lose their sense of humour, spending the rest of the day in a different way. In the beautiful sunshine of the afternoon, the opposite hill site of the city centre invited a romantic walk in a romantic setting. Benches along 'Philosophe Way' offered a rest and brilliant views across to the other side of Castle Hill. One could see down to packed roofs over the city centre and the river, also claiming its space in the valley from where they had just escaped.

While enjoying the views from a quiet distance, Martin told Arja, "Your visit pleases me so much. I'd like to keep you and not let you go away anymore. Are you cross with me because

I speak openly to you?"

Arja didn't miss these words, but still couldn't yet find the appropriate answer to it. The answer probably was that she was all smiles. Martin didn't hesitate to take things into his own hand, pulling from his pocket a shiny gold monogram ring, which he asked Arja to keep as a sign of their friendship.

Arja recalls, "Whoa! I was even more speechless and certainly blushed over my whole face listening to what else Martin had to say."

"I made that ring myself about five years ago. As you can see, it also carries my monogram.

Please take the ring with you. I want you to have it."

Indeed the ring looked beautiful and I had not the courage to give it back, but I was determined to leave it with a refusal to be kissed.

"I am not one of those that most men are after."

"You are special for me, Arja. The last thing I want is to upset you."

The next morning, the day of Arja's departure from the railway station, the weather showed its sorry face in a grey sky and drizzle. Martin accompanied her right into the train compartment, storing away her suitcase above the seat. The farewell had to be quick, because the train stopped only a few minutes in Heidelberg. Martin couldn't help saying goodbye with a hug and a kiss, which Arja didn't yet like at that time.

While the train rushed with an incredible speed northwards, the days in Heidelberg passed through her mind in pictures, as did the words that were exchanged. But not for long, as in Finland a new start at the University awaited her. The ship's passage again from Lubeck had an unpleasant surprise in store for Arja this time around. One of the numerous passengers on board the ship must have pinched her wallet while she dozed in a seat on the passenger deck. Realizing this only when getting ready to disembark from the ship in Helsinki, Arja faced the problem of how to tackle the last leg of her homecoming journey to Turku. As night fell over Helsinki, it became all the more worrisome. In the reception hall, a group of other passengers next to her discussed how to get to Turku during the night. Not hesitating, Arja joined their discussion explaining to the others her bad luck.

All four decided to fetch a taxi to Turku and share the cost between them. Said and done! In the middle of the night, Arja was dropped at her mother's place, leaving the taxi driver waiting until she returned from the flat with whatever money she could find in a hurry in a box in her room. The taxi driver gone, Arja faced an upset mother, "Why do you come back so quickly in the middle of the night, disrupting my badly needed night's sleep? What the hell can I see on your hand? Have you engaged yourself with your penfriend? I hope you haven't lost your senses and rushed into something!"

Arja was quick to respond, "No mum. I didn't rush into anything. The ring is a personal gift from Martin for our pen friendship."

"Aha, and that's it? Are you okay? That is the main thing. We had better get some sleep right now. You can tell me about your trip when I come back from work tomorrow."

The news of Arja's ring spread like wildfire. In order not to stir up more gossip outside the family, Arja took the ring off her hand, and locked it into her jewellery case. Personally, Arja was not really happy with the way she received a welcome at home just because of the ring. Her immediate reaction became not to write to Martin anymore.

The start at the University asked for all her attention so that the homecoming faded into the background sooner rather than later. In order to visit the University in Turku daily, Arja lived from then on in the city flat with her mother. The main subject at the start of her theology studies was the ancient Hebrew language in which the Christian Old Testament was written.

Arja even managed not to pay much attention to the letters from Martin. They still kept coming despite her having stopped writing. Towards the end of 1966, Martin also discontinued writing to her. Arja really didn't want this, therefore sending him a record of Finnish songs in the hope of keeping their pen friendship still alive. Martin soon wrote back. Murphy's Law had ensured her negligence at forgetting to attach her letter to the posted record disc.

Martin's letter showed plain disappointment about Arja's impersonal mail, "If you don't want to write at all any more, it's no use for me to keep writing. This makes me at least sad; what about you? Do you really want to forget our moments together? I will only write again when you have thought about our friendship and write again."

The poor 'bugger' needed consolation straight away. Arja didn't want him to suffer. To make up for her negligence, this time she did send a record disc of Maori music from Fiji in the Pacific, which she particularly liked and had received from her New Zealand pen friend. This friend had stopped writing after her fiancé tragically died in a car accident. Almost four decades later, Arja learnt from Maoris that the family name 'Kari' means 'No' in Maori language. How much did she identify herself with her name? Enough was enough. That's why she moved away from her 'no' position, cautiously writing to Martin again with time.

On the other side, Martin also answered cautiously over longer periods. A breakthrough in the sparse correspondence happened when, in early 1967, Martin informed Arja that he was going on an expedition to Asia Minor and North Africa, giving her the address of the German Embassy in Cairo, Egypt, in case she wanted to write during his absence.

What unleashed a spark in Arja, was Martin's comment, "Wouldn't it be nice if you were part of this expedition?"

For the first time Arja felt that she could lose this friendship. She became so deeply moved that she woke up, admitting to herself, "What a hell of an interesting bloke this Martin is."

Nothing could stop her writing letters anymore, the first time not in English, but in German. She couldn't help it. She was transformed in an instant. Arja's studies couldn't finish early enough so that during summer break she could go to Stockholm in Sweden to work in the quiet hope of meeting Martin again. In addition, her mum had realized the change in Arja, asking more than once, "Arja, you must be in love. Take it easy; don't rush it. We all go through this in our lives."

CHAPTER 8

Sweden – Germany – Finland/Engagement

Summer came along and Arja couldn't wait to go to Stockholm again. Taking the shipping passage became her best travel solution. She didn't forget to take Martin's ring with her in the firm hope that they would meet. This time, Arja had the address of the Salvation Army in Stockholm and she asked for work within their organisation. During this early time, Arja met up with another Finnish girl, Marja, who was about the same age, and who put in a good word for her, resulting in their working together.

Friends, Marja and Arja

The daily housework that the girls did in the organisation unmistakably showed a very different side of life. Not only was Arja unused to such a ribald lifestyle, but also she personally declined to be a part of it. Marja and she stuck together, not only during working hours but also in their time off. Sometimes the girls were called to provide room service, in which case they always went together, because quite a number of guests of this economical Salvation Army hotel had other 'ideas' about what their accommodation included. For instance, after having been occupied for a number of hours, a bathroom revealed to the service staff that a 'love party' had taken place in the bathtub. A mess of bottles surrounded the tub and all sorts of food scraps lay around on the floor. Arja had no intentions whatsoever of joining such a party.

Instead, she received red letters from Martin so regularly that hotel staff at the reception became accustomed to announcing, "Miss Arja, another red letter has arrived for you." Marja, her roommate and friend, shared the reading of the letters with her, because Arja wanted her to help write a letter in response. It was time for Arja to express her deep sympathy for her penfriend Martin. In fact, she ended up writing, "I can't help but love you so."

Both Marja and Arja were on tenterhooks, anxious to hear what Martin would write in return. They didn't have long to wait. Martin opened his heart, announcing that he would come to see Arja in Stockholm in just a few days. She was overjoyed, telling Marja how much she admired a man of such decisive power. Marja said then and many times afterwards, "What a lovely romance has developed between you two, a love story on its own!" It was set to continue over an entire lifetime.

As Arja waited for Martin to arrive in Stockholm her hope began to build as well as anxiety like never before. However, when he arrived by train at the Central Station in Stockholm, all anxiety suddenly disappeared. Martin brought sheer confidence with him. He let a bunch of red carnations tell of his initial thoughts. What followed was a kind hug from his strong arms, eyes on both sides beaming with joy, faces shining with happiness. It was so reassuring to hold each other that Arja wanted to return a kiss, which she was now ready to exchange.

Arja recalls the beauty of their time together. "Sunshine joined in our long-lasting welcome so that our day could only promise to continue on the bright side. There was so much to talk about that we didn't realize the distance we had walked through the busy city centre until we arrived at the Salvation Army Hotel. I had promised my colleague Marja that I would introduce her to Martin who had moved up the esteem-ladder straight to personal friend. Pursuing a path further along in our lives suddenly became a sincere wish for both of us. Marja congratulated me later on, "Arja, you have found luck in your life."

"Martin's stay in Stockholm was brief, but heartfelt. He could stay only until the next day, because I couldn't take more time off from my work. While resting on park benches after walking through the wide-open parts of the city, talk turned to the first serious discussions about living our lives together. I opened up to Martin, "You have become the most important person in my life. I want to share my life with you; nothing is more important than you anymore."

"Martin responded by asking, "Would you like to become my wife?" I nodded, smiled, but couldn't get a word out, so overwhelmed with happiness was I. Next morning I met Martin at the Youth Hostel where he stayed overnight. This time I brought flowers to our farewell. I thought something like that could introduce me to Martin's adoptive parents in Germany. Everything important had been said so the farewell was one of mutually strong confidence, without any anxiety at all. Our plan was simple. I would finish the couple of weeks' work in Stockholm and then take the train to Germany where Martin wanted to keep to tradition and formality and introduce me to his side of the family.

"My mum in Finland was not surprised when she heard about my plans, "You are old enough to make the right decisions for your own life. All I can hope is that everything goes well for both of you. Martin made a good impression in Finland." This was basically what mum wrote in her letter to me in Stockholm, before I took the train to Germany. The closer I came to the destination, the more anxious I became about how I would cope with an introduction to Martin's family. Of one fact, I remained assured; Martin would offer strong guidance for me.

"When the train arrived in Heidelberg, familiar bells rang so loud in my memory that I had to get out of the train to compose myself again. I used the phone, calling Martin's home further south in Ettlingen. Martin couldn't understand at first why I was calling from Heidelberg; but quickly reassured me and told me to catch the next train to the bigger city of Karlsruhe, from where he would pick me up. Regaining my courage, I caught the next train from Heidelberg. In Karlsruhe, Martin was indeed waiting for me. What a relief! The old VW bus didn't bother me. The main thing on my mind was its driver."

Martin briefly mentioned that he had a problem getting the car off his adopted father, as his adopted parents obviously were not sure about having a 'foreigner' introduced into the family. Instead, it was his friend in the neighbourhood, who lent Martin the car that they had used on their tour of Africa. Later, Arja learned that at least Martin's dad had the good grace to say, "Finns are also decent people."

Some curious members of the family had gathered to catch a glimpse of somebody from Finland. Arja's natural kindness won over most of the family, especially the older generation. In fact, Arja received special respect for speaking in German to everybody who engaged in the usual, curiosity-motivated conversation. A first 'sniff 'of the new arrival from Finland didn't last very long as her arrival took place fairly late at night. When it came to rest for the night, Martin's adopted mother went to great lengths showing Arja where she had a room of her own.

Next morning at the breakfast table Martin's adopted parents wanted to know about plans for the future. "We prefer to see Martin engaged rather than on his own, as he has repeatedly told us he preferred living his life alone. Also, he should finish his studies first before taking on responsibilities for somebody else." Arja had no say in that matter, because from Martin's account, he lived without support on his own anyway. Martin skilfully redirected the focus on celebrating our engagement here before heading to Finland. He didn't omit to point out to his stepparents that, "We came to you first, inviting you to take part in the decision of Arja and myself living our lives together. We will continue looking after ourselves as we have done up until now. You are welcome to join us in a celebration."

Doubts on the other side retreated for the time being. Martin had hit a sensitive nerve when mentioning that his adoptive parents were the first to receive personal notification of our engagement plans. Nothing should stand in the way anymore now that everybody was reassured and proud of the two young people and their decision to invite everybody in Martin's family too. It was also a good opportunity to leave behind past family discords with Martin and give the future a better chance. They had already spoken in Stockholm about this and both were in agreement.

Family members from around were notified to arrive in the afternoon for a family meeting at which the engagement would officially be announced. For her part, Arja of course, felt a bit nervous about having become the centre of interest at a family gathering at which everybody and everything was new. Her knowledge of the German language also was stretched to its limits. Luckily, there were also people present, who understood how it must feel to be the novice under scrutiny in a foreign country. They were the people to whom Arja could relate. Conversation was easier with them than others who gave the impression of having attended mainly to 'check out' the latest 'news'. If eyes could tell stories and looks could kill, Arja probably wouldn't have survived this celebration, caught somewhere between scrutiny and some degree of kindness. However, Martin stayed firmly by her side so that this examination passed, the most difficult one she had experienced so far. Martin was so important for Arja, enabling her to look past this into their own future, which they intended to build on mutual understanding.

The departure to Finland the next day couldn't come quickly enough. Martin and Arja both stood their ground, proving to themselves that they were firm in the decision to lead their lives together. In Finland, Arja's father, Petteri, received the news of the engagement too. Not having laid eyes on his future son-in-law, he had this to say, "What! Arja gets engaged to a German? This could be worse than a Russian." Petteri's memories went back to the war, when for him a Russian was bad enough. Nationality however, should be one thing, but the individual person quite another one.

Once the ship had docked in Turku harbour, Arja's dad waited with the car to pick them up, wanting to catch the first glimpse of this hopeful aspirant for his daughter's hand. Nothing untoward occurred. On the contrary, it was rather like the most natural thing in the world that these two men meet. Martin received a welcome handshake, one from a strong man's hand, which Petteri returned equally firmly and with an accepting look on his face.

Arja recalls, "Aha! I knew that Martin had passed the test of a man in Petteri's eyes. A man is a man when he can answer a challenge with strength in the broadest sense."

"Petteri continued, "You've got a nice bunch of flowers there. But in Finland men don't give flowers to each other."

"I helped out, exclaiming in Finnish, "Martin brought them all the way from Germany for Mum."

"Petteri smiled, "That's a good move with women. Flowers tell them more than men can do."

"Also on a positive note, my dad registered with satisfaction that Martin opened his address in Finnish, even if it was a bit clumsy. "Hyvaa paiva Petteri, mina olen Martin, mita kuulu? (Hello Petteri, I am Martin, how are you?)"

"The tour went from the harbour right through the city to the summerhouse in Auvaisberri. Mum had seen Martin before, accepting with joy from the bottom of her heart, a bunch of flowers, this time yellow tulips, her favourite colour. Mum responded with a hug for Martin, addressing both of us, "You both look really happy. I share your happiness." The welcome and introduction couldn't have been better. From the first days of our arrival, life continued on a regular path where everything fitted naturally together without the need to ask questions. I realized that Martin had already won the hearts of Mum and Dad. Notwithstanding a call for family unity, mum and dad put their differences aside, attaching greater importance to my future.

"A couple of days passed in a holiday atmosphere, including a typical introduction to sauna, swimming, boating, fishing, collecting berries in the forest, seeing neighbours and friends and, while in the city, shopping for our engagement rings. Before the weekend, a festivity for only the closest family members began. A dinner table illuminated by candlelights invited Mum and Dad to join us on the veranda. It was still daylight for hours more, well into the late night, offering views across parts of the lake framed by dark green pine forested islands.

"Food of every type that Finland could offer was finely presented: fish, meats, potatoes, noodles, salads, stews, berries, and fruit (mainly apples, imported dark and white grapes mixed in with a banana or an orange that were not yet easy to get at that time). A selection of glasses for champagne, wine, beer or liquors accompanied each plate during the course of our dinner. All four of us were dressed in our 'glad rags', in which Mum especially looked so wonderful, almost juvenile as if celebrating her own engagement. The fluffy, flowery, silk-like summer costume accentuated her joyfulness, not showing the slightest sign of the past years' struggles since the divorce from Dad.

Petteri's favourite pastime in 1967

"On that day, everything negative was left behind. Mum and Dad received my decision to share my life with Martin with open arms. Petteri added his strong, characteristic humour to our festive evening. Off went the cork of the champagne bottle with a loud bang, right up to the ceiling, but not spilling one drop of its sweet refreshment as it poured into one glass after another. The moment had then arrived where, in line with family tradition, the new son-in-law formally asked the parents to agree to the proposal of marriage with their daughter.

"May I ask you, Tysse and Petteri, for your daughter Arja's hand in marriage?"

"Martin had prepared himself for the occasion, asking this question in Finnish. The excitement, however, took its toll on him. He became stuck with the sentence, looking to me for support and we finished the sentence together. Mum and Dad on the opposite side of the table were all smiles, nodding their heads and lifting their glasses. Encouraging us to follow, this simply meant, "Yes, we would love to give our consent."

"Mum and Dad kept our gold engagement rings, handing one to each of us in turn. Firstly, they witnessed Martin placing his ring on to the ring finger of my left hand and then I repeated the same on his left hand. A kiss of the betrothed sealed the ring ceremony. The party started then, continuing well into the early hours of the following day over dinner, drinks, Finnish songs, German songs contributed by Martin and last, but not least English songs by the younger generation.

"Later during the festivity, Petteri secretly mixed some of the heavier 'stuff' into Martin's drinks in order to check out how the new son-in-law would stand up when eventually getting drunk. Petteri, of course, encouraged Martin to drink along with him, which Mum and I didn't do. As Martin never was a drinker, he was not spared realizing that the drinks took away his normal well-being. Therefore, he stopped just in time, which signalled to Petteri that Martin was a man not likely to lose control. Despite this test receiving positive marks, the party came to a halt soon after in order to get fit again for the following day. There was to be an official dinner in the city's most exclusive restaurant.

"Martin had his accommodation in the room under the gables. The next morning he told me that the aftermath of the mixed drinks caught up with him the moment he lay down on the bed. "I just reached the window in time to empty my stomach out the window before returning to bed, sick and sorry to try to find some sleep." The result of this was that, not only Martin but also Mum were too sick to go out for another dinner the following day. Petteri didn't fail to exclaim, "Here we are; who are the strong and who are the weak ones?"

"The close family engagement party, however, remained a success, despite these shortcomings. What came next was a festivity with the wider circle of family and friends joining us in an official celebration. Looking back today to my engagement, I sincerely hope that such traditions will not be lost in the future. Increasingly, young people turn their back on tradition, avoiding commitments without knowing with what to replace it. We can never know what lies ahead in our lives. What we can do is to commit ourselves to a partner in life, constantly exercising mutual respect, tolerance, encouragement and forgiveness. In such a close relationship with one's real life partner, two people can strive for and achieve common goals and satisfaction in good as well as bad times. People abandoning this will experience the down sides of life without finding an anchoring place to be rescued from one's 'ego'. During life, it *will always be the other person that can unleash new efforts in us for common benefits in our walk through life.*

"I hope that my life story won't lose a common understanding in the future. People have to ask themselves how life is now if the simple senses of life are lost. It could amount to a loss of our existence when people cannot experience the excitement of building on commitment during a lifespan. A known fact is also that no 'good' can be achieved without having experienced challenges - the 'less good' but not necessarily the 'bad'.

"Let me return to the official day of our engagement. Mainly the younger generation of relatives and friends in Finland turned up. One cousin brought along a guitar, which led to an exchange of songs and guitar music. Some of them might have come to see the man who had managed to change my mind about never getting married. There is a saying, 'Where love falls down, there is no remedy for it.' However, if love keeps growing under protection, it can flourish into an individual expression, often nurtured at first in secrecy. Everything in life starts small and doesn't necessarily become visible at all times. Such love can develop in its own 'nest' under individual protection.

"A more open, informal party took place in and around the house. The day passed quickly in a cross-section of languages: conversations in Finnish, English, or German, depending on personal preferences, ensured that everyone could be a part of our day. Everybody had arrived one by one at different times during the morning and gradually took off again, leaving us alone to consider the next step in our new lives together.

"For me, this move became the most important one of my life. Martin had to continue his studies in Heidelberg, but I didn't want to stay back in Finland. Life with Martin had changed my search for direction instantly into just one. I had woken from my world of skepticism. It must have been real love, receiving assurances about one's life from someone else and leaving uncertainty behind. Trust is the substance of it all, which took its own time in our relationship to build certainty out of uncertainty. The concept of a 'honeymoon' meant, in our case, Finland became our 'honeymoon'. We felt committed to each other, but still maintained some 'doors' to open later. At that moment, reality knocked on our door, asking to respond in a way that life could continue for both of us together.

CHAPTER 9

First Life Together in Germany

The first step in Martin and Arja's journey was to return to Germany. They intended to return the same way they had come, firstly by boat through the Baltic Sea and then by train to the south of Germany. Arja's mother visibly shared their happiness, but couldn't hide the tears that ran down her cheeks during the couple's farewell from Finland. The realities of life immediately tested Martin and Arja's readiness to find solutions for all kinds of problems: where to live, what to do for a living and how to fit in their plans for their future together.

The two of them had to stay in Martin's stepparents' place for a day, just until they had found the direction they wanted to go. It was good to keep this dependency as short as possible in order to avoid inquisitiveness and a mixed understanding from occurring again. A good personal standard of independence has always been the key for good relationships with others. The door to other people's 'homes' often costs an 'entry fee' which has the mark of the host in the first place.

Sometime earlier, Arja had submitted her application for nurse's training to a hospital in the nearby larger city of Karlsruhe. The response waited for them at Martin's home address and invited Arja to present herself on her arrival in Germany. Deaconess Hospital of Ruppurr accepted the application and started her immediately with ward work. The housing facility for hospital staff within the hospital complex solved the immediate problem of board and lodging. Generally, the atmosphere in the hospital was of a friendly nature with the usual one or two exemptions. In this case, one or two older nursing staff didn't like a young trainee nurse being so easily engaged.

"You need your undivided attention for your hospital career, just like I've done to get myself to a leading, responsible position."

Arja had no problem with such a statement, but still reserved the right to run her private life her own way, with her fiancé meeting her on weekends, sometimes in Heidelberg and sometimes in Karlsruhe. A similar message to that of the hospital came from Martin's adoptive parents, "You should not distract Martin from his studies; you better leave him alone." Arja accepted this message too, because she knew that Martin had looked after his own life for a number of years already, never receiving any support that could have justified listening to his parents.

For almost one year, Martin and Arja went on like this, meeting on weekends after a week's work. Martin again lost some serious study time at the University in Heidelberg because of open disputes with the Baader-Meinhoff group. Arja continued to do her part at the hospital to the best of her abilities and was successful at her work. However, she could not help, but feel increasingly that she was just a tolerated foreigner.

The nuns, who were nurses, especially seemed to have a problem with her. They often reprimanded Arja, "You are here just to learn how to do nursing and nothing else. Patients are not here to talk to you."

Arja simply could not relax in such an environment and together with Martin, after one year, they made the decision that she would move to Heidelberg and take on studies rather than continue in the Deaconess Hospital. Arja's departure from the hospital went without problems, as she hadn't signed any in-house agreement yet. Luckily, it was before the end of the first service year, which ran anyway on a probation period.

CHAPTER 10

Tying the 'Knot'

Early in the summer of 1968, Martin and Arja received news from Finland that Arja's sister planned to get married in August. She suggested a double-marriage, "The eleventh of August will be your engagement anniversary so why not also get married on the same day one year later?"

Meanwhile, Martin and Arja had plenty of opportunities to experience the rules for non-married couples at that time: no joint accommodation for unmarried couples. Even at the University hostel in Heidelberg, married couples were bound to live separately in hostel facilities. What a strange world to live in? People usually move from one extreme to another opposite one, which only proves, we rarely know what we are really doing. Martin and Arja, however, knew exactly what they did and didn't want.

Only a few years later, the 'doors' were opened wide, allowing everybody to mix and live together as one, backed by a newly implemented 'non-discriminatory rule'. In other words, what had been a strict rule before was reluctantly thrown out and nothing replaced it instead. The fallout of this 'easy liberalism' application can be seen in many ways today and certainly will be more accentuated in the future.

Loss of discipline was probably the most notable result. Discipline is a basis for everything where learning is required, so this was a change with far reaching consequences.

The world has always been good at throwing something out, but rarely finding a suitable replacement for it. Married or not, when Arja moved to Heidelberg, it became obvious to her that antiquated rules were bent anyway, resulting in mixed accommodation. Already there was a dominant rule in place, "Make sure, you don't get caught." There were plenty of people around helping themselves by adhering to such an 'avoidance scheme' in all sorts of life situations. This didn't apply for Martin and Arja though, because if wanting some degree of individual control over one's life, both sides have to be transparent and accountable to the other side. Within reason, it is important not to provoke mistrust, from where all 'bad things' start.

Arja's matriculation at Heidelberg University, the oldest established University in the world, went forward, as Finnish education standards were, and still are, fully recognized in Germany. While one hurdle was overcome, the answers to the question of a double marriage in August in Finland came in. With the help of the young couple, Arja's mother wrote an invitation to Martin's stepparents in German. They received it positively, not resisting another opportunity to tell them, "We'd rather see Martin married than leading his life on his own."

A week before the marriage date of August 11, 1968, everybody drove to Finland for the occasion. What a surprise it was that no conditions attached to our decision were first presented. This, however, didn't last long as the well intended recommendations admonished both Martin and Arja. Martin's parents almost continuously brought up their feelings of doubt. The first days of the month of August saw the two students leave behind some of the headaches of student life in Heidelberg, at least temporarily. However, there was still the trip with Martin's parents to Finland. The weather fortunately didn't hesitate to show its sunny side during the eighteen hundred kilometres to Finland.

In those days, it was still a firm tradition that the bride's parents invited the guests and organized the wedding. Progress in future years saw many discarding this 'rule' as efforts were increasingly measured with money and the same 'rule' fell short on the account of aspirations of living standards. Arja's parents in Finland pulled together in their efforts in a time essential for the family. Even though they had divorced, unity had priority over past discords.

Petteri and Arja, Telakka/Turku, 1968

The beautiful weather and the happy atmosphere between the four travellers prevailed despite a potentially dangerous incident. While driving on the first leg to Stockholm, the VW caravan nearly hit an obstacle on the side of the road. If Martin had not corrected the steering from his side seat in time, an accident would surely have ensued. His dad, the driver, turned furious for no obvious reason. However, with time everyone calmed down and all was friendly again when boarding the ship, which was to carry them across the Baltic Sea to Turku in

Finland. For Arja and Martin, the passage was already a familiar one, whereas Martin's parents couldn't believe there was sunbathing on the deck of the ship still after 10 pm. They were also fascinated to watch the sun near the horizon sending red lights across a curled glittering ocean surface, which shelters a unique archipelago of forested islands. The islands varied in size from those with just a few northern pines right up to the larger islands.

Martin's parents enjoyed this picture-book passage tremendously, which ensured they were at ease for the welcome in Finland. The sharp spire of the Turku Castle Tower appeared on the horizon, announcing the passage would soon be over. Once the ship had anchored parallel to the pier, a large part of the city could be seen from the upper decks, a height of at least a ten-storey building. The views surpassed most buildings and entered far into the streets that led to the harbour. One could see that after crossing a rail passage of massive crane structures, service buildings stretched low along the quay, parallel to the anchored ship down at the end of the landing bridge.

Arja joyfully remembers the welcome. "Mum, Dad, my sister with her fiancé; they all waited to welcome us. Dad Petteri spontaneously took the initiative by breaking the formality of the situation with an introduction by dancing arm in arm with Martin. Martin's parents were simply speechless, their mouths open in surprise at such unperturbed action, probably not recognizing their son any more in the company of my family. My mum concealed her face behind a bunch of flowers, welcoming Martin's parents by anxiously speaking a welcome in German, "Willkommen in Finland (Welcome in Finland)".

"With such a full, fiery welcome, the 'ice' didn't even have time to form let alone have a need to be broken. Only smiles could be seen on everybody's faces. Mum entrusted her city flat solely to the personal use of Martin's parents, giving them the freedom to move freely around on their own. They could get to know a little bit of Finland, a country they hadn't been to before. For their part, they liked what they saw. Martin's dad even went to great lengths, driving up north to Tampere in Middle Finland and then to the east to Helsinki. From what he said, his impressions were

all good. As a 'serious' paper-manufacturing engineer, he didn't miss paying visits to some Finnish manufacturing plants, all this without letting anybody else know about it. For that reason, they nearly missed the wedding day's bell ringing.

"A festive event unfolded for the families, friends, neighbours, and acquaintances from the public, school and out of the business world. Everybody had arrived in their glad rags witnessing the double marriage of my parents' only two daughters. Grandma from Pispala insisted on her presence too. She arrived two days earlier in order to see for herself how I took this important step in my life, committing myself to sharing the ups and downs with a partner for life. She saw Martin for the first time, expressing her satisfaction upon his cautious, but friendly appearance towards the older generation of the family. The few Finnish words Martin used in his address pleased grand mum in particular. She felt mutual sympathy from the first moment expressing herself to me, "Arja, you have chosen a good husband. The nationality doesn't really matter, as long as the person is honest and therefore also good."

"Martin had been baptized in Christian Lutheran tradition, the main religion in Finland, so that the pastor of the dome of Turku received our congregation. My father Petteri ushered his two daughters arm in arm, each one at his side, down the centre passage to the far end of the church. Here, in front of the altar the pastor waited with the grooms, each one at his side, to receive the brides out of the hands of Petteri. All guests stood up from their bench seats as the pastor opened his speech in German much to the surprise of Martin's parents. The ceremony ended with one partner receiving one ring at a time from the pastor to be placed on the right ring finger. This was then repeated with the other partner. Brides and grooms then exchanged the official kiss, which released everybody from the official side of the ceremony. For my part, I did not feel nervous at all, as I had heard that other brides did. On the contrary, our eyes and hands met so calmly in front of the altar, setting the seal on our deepest wishes.

Petteri leading his two daughters

The two brides and grooms, Turku, 1968

"The day before the wedding, when a number of acquaintances had come to the summerhouse in Auvaisberri to see the newly 'imported' groom, an incident caused a 'cosmetic' headache for Martin. Beside a billiard table in the attic of the house was a swing mounted on to the roof rafters. For some unexplained reason, the swing somehow ended in Martin's mouth, knocking out two teeth. Consequently, a dentist received a late afternoon visit to correct as quickly as possible (and of course expensively) the good looks of Martin. In that sense, our marriage was 'saved' by a dentist.

"After the ceremony, the party could go ahead without reservations. The large number of guests could assemble only in large premises, so we ended up inside a special school. Conversations and cocktails kept the party going, giving the opportunity for people to get to know each other better. This was important, as most guests had seen neither Martin nor his parents before. Where the language seemed to block a conversation, I reluctantly helped out, which kept me on my toes. I felt good assisting my parents-in-law to feel at home in Finland and not have to worry about language problems. My parents-in-law also spoke some Hungarian, which they had learned at school during the time when Transylvania had been occupied by Hungary, which was where Martin and his adoptive parents came from. Slightly disappointed, they discovered that they were not able to understand one Finnish word despite the theory that Finnish and Hungarian are supposed to have the same 'Finnish-Ugric' origin. In my later life, when in Hawaii with Martin, the real connection from early migrations became clear: Hawaiian to Hokkaido-Japanese to Finnish. The only similarity is in the many vowels, long words and accentuation of the first syllables of words.

"One of the highlights of this official party became a dance with the two newly married couples starting first. The bride and groom then exchanged partners with the parents-in-law until everybody danced across the parquetry to the sound of record music. Late in the afternoon, the party dispersed, leaving only the newly married couples to join the parents in moving to their corresponding homes. My sister went to the home of her husband's parents whereas our party gathered in my father's newly acquired boat-building place, where he had prepared a cottage for Martin and I to stay in.

"It was late at night on the wedding day when Martin and I retreated from our families' continuing party. As we entered the cottage, I found a neighbourhood man had already settled in the cottage. Was this meant to be a joke? Anyway, I was the first to go up the stairs into our room and when I realized that somebody else occupied the bed, I became determined to send the stranger 'to the devil'. At first, in the darkness of the room, the other person was difficult to recognize. I was a bit frightened at first, but soon turn more determined, "You get out of here! What are you doing here?" In his state of drunkenness the bloke moved towards the door shaken and responding, "You will become a 'sergeant' of a wife for a poor husband." 'Sergeant', poor or not, I sent him packing in less than a minute.

"The next day, 'rumours' had already found their way around town, saying that the bride had 'brutally' thrown out a homeless man from the nuptial bed. However, isn't it said, "That no man can serve two masters?" The same ought also to apply to a woman. This was and still is my view. Any 'rumour' not eliciting the expected response, disappears as quickly as it started and so did this one. Life the next day already moved back to a routine from where a newly married couple could get on with their own lives.

"A few more days in Finland allowed us to see some of the other people who couldn't take part in the wedding celebration for some reason. For a few, the message didn't reach them in time. My colleagues from the local university for instance, also received a visit to the campus. At an informal gathering, they teased, "Aha, this is our new Arja, who was so obstinately set against considering a male friend."

"Only the right one had to turn up," was my reply. "Everything in life needs its own time."

"From now on, I couldn't argue with my parents-in-law who didn't want to miss the opportunity while in Finland to look around a bit more as far as Helsinki to the east. Martin's dad couldn't help informing himself on the spot about Finnish paper manufacturing standards, which has been his professional occupation over a lifespan. According to him, what he saw impressed him. "Indeed, the Finns are very progressive, matching anybody around the world." This was from somebody who convincingly spoke about Germany.

"Martin had previously mentioned to me that his adopted father had always tried to win him over to his profession of a Chemistry Engineer. Martin steadily refused to accept this argument. Could it have been the case that, while in Finland, Martin's father saw a 'backdoor' to getting Martin interested in paper manufacturing, even at this late stage of his father's life? It didn't work, however, as previous discord couldn't be forgotten that quickly. I found that in Martin's case, being an adopted child more readily caused discord. In a generation, change lay more heavily on both parties than if a direct family descent were the case. Such discord unfortunately caught up even with me in coming years, despite my having no previous contacts with Martin's parents. However, we were both determined not to give in to outside interference in our lives.

"To this day, Martin and I have not only overcome all the odds against us, but have succeeded to such an extent that forty years later we are still sharing our life together. To listen in tolerance to each other, has been the one essential key to our extraordinary lives. Demanding and trying to enforce one's own way of thinking, rather keeps 'doors' to each other shut and it wouldn't make sense to live with somebody who was like this. It would result only in constant disagreements as this can be experienced around us more than one would like to admit. I've seen this happen to my parents and if Martin hadn't shown a straightforward character with a good measure of adaptation towards the lives of two people from very different backgrounds we might not have found each other. It wouldn't have convinced me to accept sharing everything during our lifespan."

"It took Martin a while to 'melt the ice' surrounding Arja. But in the process of adaptation was firmly imbedded Finnish 'sisu' (cautious determination) and once this is unleashed in a Finn, that's it. Finns stick to this determination and make life work, no matter what may come. Why Martin's parents didn't stop criticizing and condemning Arja, even after they had taken part in their wedding in Finland, developed into a source of regret towards the end of their lives. On a trip to Germany from their home in Australia, Martin and Arja visited Martin's mother who was already ninety. She said, "You must be a unique couple. All the ups and downs we have witnessed in your lives have only strengthened your commitment to each other. You are still happily together with your own family of six children while so many others, even in our extended family, have separated, turning their back on their commitments. I have to admit that I misjudged both of you for too long."

There is at least one secret in dealing with other people, including the extended family that we can choose our friends but not necessarily our family members. There is a saying, 'A soup is never that hot when eaten, as it comes off the stove'. This means that the one who can wait is less likely to eat his soup while it is still too hot. This became Arja's attitude, which her parents-in-law couldn't understand. She always stayed neutral, even when overhearing statements of conflict and never dug in her heels to battle, who was right or wrong. Over the years, Martin and Arja kept up contact with Martin's parents despite some very unpleasant incidents amounting almost to racism.

Arja has been the first 'foreigner' in Martin's whole extended family and possibly because of that, constituted a bit too much of a challenge for them all. People can usually act only on what they do know, and mostly out of insecurity, distance themselves. They don't see that people are not so different from each other. It is the language, nationality and borders creating the divide and whoever gets caught in those aspects divides himself from other people. In many respects, Martin's parents must have deprived themselves greatly by what they claimed to know. Many times over, Martin and Arja overlooked their responses for the good of the wider family. It was different in Finland where they could count on support, enabling them to look past the sorry state of relations with Martin's parents. This was not always easy, but stepping back from family conflict, secured their freedom. 'An eye for an eye, and a tooth for a tooth' was never the young couple's philosophy as it is not a good way of maintaining freedom.

After the wedding in Finland, Arja, Martin and his parents returned to Germany the same way they had come over. Almost everybody they had seen during the two weeks in Finland turned up at the quay in the harbour of Turku to say goodbye. The huge passenger ship took the car and them on board after a hearty farewell from everybody. Nobody could have missed the emotional excitement that Finland had given everyone and even Arja's new 'in-laws' became visibly moved too, despite the language barrier. At least the excitement lasted for the duration of the trip back to the south of Germany. Because of the distance that had to be covered by car, it should have necessitated changing drivers regularly. However, Martin's father insisted on doing all the driving. Martin could not even offer to drive, as some unexplained stubbornness kept his adoptive father uncompromisingly at the wheel. Martin knew it was more important to keep the peace, giving them a better chance of a return of goodwill. Eventually, everybody arrived in one piece. The 'old man' at sixty-six still regarded Martin at twenty-seven as a childish youth who, in his view, hadn't learnt enough yet.

Why this was so remained an open question. Then, what about Arja? At the age of twenty-three, was it with her that their problem started? All problems aside though, action became the priority after having returned first to Martin's parents' home for a short time. Neither Martin nor Arja wanted to stay one day longer than was absolutely necessary.

CHAPTER 11

Life Between Germany and Finland

After returning from the wedding in Finland, Martin and Arja's lives were to continue together, firstly in Heidelberg. Usually, students in those days didn't possess much that would hinder their moving. Room accommodation for students in Heidelberg was very difficult to get because in 1968 America still had its military corps stationed in Heidelberg. From here, they would be transferred to the raging war in Vietnam. Military personnel were heavily subsidized to live in local accommodation outside the military compounds. This turned the rental market upside down, making it expensive beyond most students' means. To find that roof over your head, a bed, and a table and chair was difficult, but the student dwelling houses did the trick for the newly married couple.

At that time, there was a rule still in place that male and female students were accommodated in separate buildings regardless of whether they were married or not. It didn't take long for Martin and Arja to find out that such solo accommodation didn't serve the purpose of serious studies very well. Personally, Arja discovered from other students how they went about their private life, which encouraged Martin and her to quickly look for private room accommodation. It took only a short time after having moved into separate buildings to make this decision.

Neither Martin nor Arja considered themselves as 'living in the dark ages', but what came to their attention in some student circles, only supported their desire to move out of these surroundings. Martin, for instance, had to enforce a rule with his colleague. "During the night, I want to sleep and you must keep your female visitors away. While I am at the Uni during the day you can have your 'sleepover' with whoever you want, but not while I am present." Arja encountered a similar scenario. Her female room colleague occasionally had a laugh about Arja, not hesitating to call her friends and have a laugh together at her. "Look at this model student who needs to be married to have sex with only one partner. You'd better join us and not stay aside."

Arja acknowledged that people surely are different, "But that didn't stop Martin and me having our own freedom of choice in our lives. Others could have whatever they wanted, as long as respecting other's views too. More than once, we returned to our rooms and after opening the door, closed it again quickly to check the room number. To be polite, we left and ignored what we saw. Obviously, for some, studies extended to sex instruction even during the daytime. If only they knew how sidetracked they got in their lives by losing focus on their own goals. Like so many times in life, luck often switches position."

To earn some extra money, Martin occasionally umpired tennis tournaments. During such an occasion, a woman approached him, asking whether he was 'so and so'. This resulted in the discovery that Marion, the lady tennis player, was a relative of Martin's parents. This alone was, of course, nothing worth talking about, except that she mentioned that she was moving out of private student accommodation into something that she thought was better. At the end of the tournament, over a cup of tea, addresses were exchanged and Martin received assurance that Marion would put in a good word for them with her present landlady. Luck was on our side; the landlady immediately received our personal presentation plus a reference from Marion. Her recommendation helped ensure that the couple could move into something more like their own home. At the time, this was an achievement not to be underestimated, considering the Heidelberg rental market.

Heidelberg accommodation, 1969

The place turned out, on one hand, to be very small and old, but it had also its good points. It was close to everything in the city and quietly located in the backyard of surrounding tenement houses. A green foreshore of the river Neckar, just a stone's throw from where they lived, supplied some good spaces for walks, and this was virtually opposite the crowded city centre. All the furniture - bookshelves, bed, table, chairs - Martin either quickly made himself on site, or made the rounds to second hand shops to get a good deal. Other people often throw out so much good stuff, which at the time was a sign of a rising living standard for them both.

For the remaining time of the summer study break, Martin earned good money as a machine salesman, making also deals on the side like the one that brought them two beautiful Persian carpets into the new home. With oil paintings on the walls, the place was ready for the house-warming party. Marion, of course, was the first guest and surprisingly many more friends and acquaintances turned up for the occasion. Arja did her part by baking pastry in their specially acquired stove, which without doubt pleased everybody. Their Heidelberg home was a success, at least for the time being.

Often when life nears its best, the opposite is not far away, waiting to move in. Their studies meanwhile went ahead, leaving very little time after some extra work, which had to be squeezed in to pay for life's expenses. Besides her studies at the Foreign Language Institute, Arja helped out for a few hours daily in a household, looking after the family's two small children. Martin, on the other hand, earned the money they needed mainly during term breaks with his technical profession from where he intended gradually to move into an alternate profession.

From early on, Martin mentioned feeling a bit uncertain about the future, the new direction in his life. He knew he could earn better money during his breaks than he possibly could have hoped with a change in his profession. At a certain stage, Martin had to abandon his Medicine studies because the fees were too high for him to find on top of living costs. Strangely enough, he also was denied a student subsidy, following an investigation. According to the investigators, Martin's stepparents were wealthy enough to support their son, even though they never had. Martin had enough of the bureaucrats' bungling and decided to return to his profession of engineer.

Now and then, narrow escapes financially in our daily life were overcome just in time, usually with unconditional help from faraway Finland. Although Arja's life story has moved now into events of our lives together, she continues to tell her side of the story as it happened in her eyes. Martin had later written a book, "Journey of a Lifetime, Volume 2," which starts after our engagement in Germany. The whole theme of that book would be how two initially very different personalities from two very different countries came to build their lives together, succeeding against all the odds.

A discussion about our future took an interesting turn on a cold, snowy and sunny Sunday during winter in early 1969. The weather invited an outing on foot into the snow-capped forest that creeps up the hill sites, not far from where we lived. Arja began to feel a bit dizzy and therefore couldn't keep pace with Martin. Suddenly her strength abandoned her and if Martin hadn't caught her instantly in his arms, she might have fallen to the ground.

After a few moments in which Arja regained consciousness, Martin asked her, "Is something wrong with you, Arja?" At first, she couldn't say anything, because she too was taken by surprise. However, after a few more moments Arja put her head on Martin's shoulder, whispering in his ear, "I am expecting our child."

Martin held her still firmer, looking with a smile into her eyes, "This is wonderful! Our lives have taken on a new direction. We are holding to what we promised ourselves. We want wild celebrations!" Arja found it easy to return his smile.

The excursion, however, stopped then at that spot in the wintry forest; their pace turned slowly back home. The 'die was cast'. Martin did not hesitate one moment more about how our future would go. His studies ended in coming months and he and Arja both happily agreed to prepare ourselves for our family life. It clearly pointed in the direction of our higher expectations.

Arja testing the cot, 1969

A local, precision instrumentation, manufacturing company interviewed Martin only a few weeks before the baby was due to arrive. Martin not only could secure employment straight away but also new lodgings were available through the company. Arja recalls a strange incident with the landlady, who ran her own private kindergarten.

"She sent us a registered letter from a holiday place in Austria, demanding we leave the premises without delay, since we were expecting a child. We had no answer to why this sudden decision came out of the blue. Anyway, where there is a will there is a way.

"After Martin had secured the new accommodation with the company owner, a report appeared on the front page of the biggest newspaper in Germany, "Bild-Zeitung." On the front page, an article reported about a kindergarten teacher who couldn't stand one child living in her own rented dwellings. As none of the lessors could be contacted, Martin also brought our case to the attention of the Landlords'

Association, which accepted that we bring forward our case at their public meeting during which answers certainly would have emerged.

"Apparently, on hearing about our moves, the kindergarten landlady all of a sudden appeared in front of our door, exclaiming excitedly, "All this must be a misunderstanding. If you refrain from appearing at the Landlords' Association Meeting, you can stay as long as you like."

"Thank you for your 'kindness', but we have already made our arrangements to comply with your request. If you agree, we will move out in two days, also leaving the case unpursued." No matter what we tried, our two children whom we had in Germany were only a 'stumbling block' for others, who either had no children or had forgotten that they also were once children.

Arja with Risto, Heidelberg, 1970

"Despite all the 'economic miracles' of Germany and its 'progress', it was a struggle in this environment for parents and their children to find a place in society. In fact, a rental situation for a family with small children was at the time so difficult that we felt like lepers. Accommodation ads expressed, without hesitation, "Families with children need not apply." On the other hand, dogs and cats rarely got a mention at all. What future can people have if they don't feel comfortable with young families *amidst a society? We left it to others to find the answer while we worked on a solution that would better serve our needs.*

Every so often, we visited my family in Finland. On one occasion, we also moved back there with all our belongings just to find out whether or not to call Finland our home. The accommodation problem wouldn't have existed in Finland for us. However, Martin's lack of Finnish, even with his best efforts, could not meet employment standards satisfactorily. Mainly, it was Martin, who didn't want to be a burden for the others in the family. The reason we didn't search long for possibilities in Finland was probably because I was much too excited at the prospect of living far away in a warmer country."

Residential block, Karlsruhe-Germany, 1971

Petteri and Risto, Finland 1972

Arja with Raija and Risto, Karlsruhe, 1971

CHAPTER 12

Life in South Africa

South Africa had accepted Martin and Arja's application and so a new direction opened in their lives. To Arja, in her drive for new horizons, Africa sounded magical. In August 1972, Martin travelled on his own to take up a professional appointment in the surroundings of Johannesburg. There were, of course, hurdles in the different world of Africa and this caused Martin to write rather sceptically about the move to Africa. However, Arja reassured him because she wanted to see the world too.

Arja found that the three months in Finland could not pass quickly enough. She boarded the long distance flight to South Africa with her three children. Arja recalls, "Our third child was born during those three months in Finland with the first snow of winter. I was well looked after and when my departure day arrived, sadness mixed with joy marked the faces of my extended family in Finland. It was sadness that we went so far away, but joy about our spirit of enterprise. My dad didn't know that when he had farewelled Martin by saying, "I won't see this bloke anymore," that he would be so right. Sadly, my father was to be the one saying good-bye with his life before another two years went by.

During the three months of my stay in Finland, Martin had organized everything in South Africa - work, our own house and everything else. I touched down in the beginning of December at Jan Smuts Johannesburg International Airport. I had never been on such a long flight in such a big aircraft, crossing the whole of Europe first and then the vast African continent. I had never before experienced such an incredibly sun-flooded, crystal-clear sky, which prepared a homecoming for our family. During the long hours of the flight, the children kept me busy. However, knowing our family was to be reunited swept away all tiredness, at least for the time being.

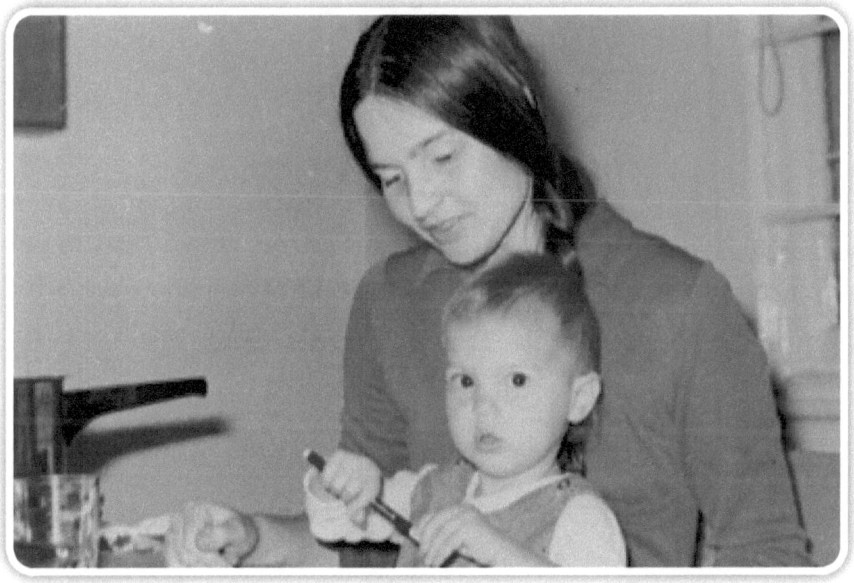

Arja with daughter Raija, Xmas 1972, Krugersdorp, South Africa

Blauberg Strand, Cape Town, Raija and Risto, 1973

At the time, South Africa well and truly met our expectations, in fact far more than we had hoped for. There were plenty of opportunities for qualified people along with good incomes and very low tax deductions. Weekends saw our family making wonderful excursions into the harsh, but beautiful African countryside. Nature in abundance was evident in the roaming wildlife - lions, elephants, zebras, giraffes, wildebeests, rhinos and many other species. Unparalleled sunny weather guaranteed that virtually every weekend was spent in outdoor living."

Social unrest, however, impetuously clouded the South African land, turning the country into a minefield of internal conflict with immeasurable consequences. It was unlike anything that we, Martin and Arja had ever experienced. In addition, we believed that the situation as we found it in South Africa was a relic of the past, left unchanged for too long and thereby taking unwanted directions. This especially became evident in the escalating crime rate.

Martin and Arja made a joint decision, not out of fear, but out of considered personal judgement that after three years in South Africa we would move somewhere else. We both wanted to leave the mounting, politically motivated problems behind. In a way, it was a pity to have to make that decision, considering the good life they experienced in South Africa. There were never, ever any complaints about children. On the contrary, children seemed to represent an important asset for African society. The focus was on their lives and they were accepted regardless of societal background. Were the children of South Africa the forerunners in abolishing 'apartheid'? On the other hand, had progress in different parts of Europe, from where we had come, turned against its own people by forgetting that it is the children who will follow in the prepared footsteps of a society?

Blauberg Strand, Cape Town, the whole family, 1973

CHAPTER 13

Life in Brazil

During an earlier visit when Martin and Arja still lived in Germany, relatives of Martin who lived in Brazil asked them, "Why don't you come to Brazil?" This question resurfaced when a move away from South Africa was imminent. In 1975, it took just a few months to gain migration acceptance to Brazil for our whole family.

Besides preparations to move to Brazil, efforts to learn the Portuguese language were given high priority. Language is the key for a smooth integration into any other country. Daily systematic listening to a language course, while dozing in bed every night, helped enormously. Within three months, Martin and Arja could speak Portuguese well enough so that when we showed up at the Embassy, we could already converse quite well. More refined learning of the language followed easily once we actually lived in the country.

The way we ran our lives was based on mutual discussions. Once an agreement could be reached, Arja supported the husband all the way, which included letting the children take part in family decisions as well. While in South Africa, another family member 'turned up'. This meant that there was now a balance of two girls and two boys. Brazil was and is a country where children have a say in the society, making opinions from every Brazilian important.

Proof of that was delivered the moment the family stepped into a Brazilian airliner, which took us on a highly dangerous mission. The plane had to make a detour through Luanda, the capital of Angola, before heading west, directly towards Brazil. Angola was then under siege by rebels, turning the stopover in Luanda into a risky adventure. The military had to secure the runway of the airport with armed forces for the landing and take-off.

A large number of refugees, who obviously could afford to pay, were squeezed into the Boeing 707. Everybody had to take one person on his or her lap, virtually double loading the aircraft with passenger numbers. Martin and Arja later learnt that Brazil makes almost anything possible. The aircraft, under tank protection all along the runway, took off, continuing without problems to its destination of Rio de Janeiro. During the flight, the children could move around freely and were even invited into the cockpit to see the pilots.

Brazil did not wait to introduce itself with 'amisada' (amusement), as Brazilians would have called it. Nothing seems to be taken too seriously, a necessary balance in Brazilian life, which our family was about to experience on landing in the middle of the night in the mega-city of Rio de Janeiro. The connecting flight to Sao Paulo, another Brazilian mega-city situated on the Brazilian plateau further south, had already left. The delayed arrival of the previous flight left a considerable number of people stranded, including Martin, Arja and our children.

Arja recalls, "On the tarmac, a number of aircraft waited, not knowing whether or not they were ready to take passengers on or rest idle for the night. Within the confusion about where the plane to Sao Paulo might be, people rather engaged in 'amisada' with our children to help the time pass. The issue of which was the right plane and when it was leaving remained a problem. Everybody had to find out for himself as nobody could say for sure just who was ground personnel and who was a passenger.

"Asking questions and slowly getting answers showed that nobody was in a hurry. "How do we get from here to Sao Paulo tonight?"

"No problem, just follow us. One of these planes is waiting to take us on."

"Do you know for sure that the plane we are boarding is the one to Sao Paulo?"

"Don't worry, it will get us there."

"How do we know the plane is going to Sao Paulo?"

"I am pretty sure. Soon we will find out."

"In fact, inside the plane an attractive flight attendant with her bright smile and big, dark eyes shining out of a beautiful, chocolate coloured face confirmed it. "You are welcome. We are about to take off to Sao Paulo. You have nice children. Where do you come from? Leave the children with me. Our on-board personnel will look after them. Relax, our flight will take only one hour."

Fiery samba music on board the plane got us on the way into the dark sky leaving the city lights behind. They were taken over by silent darkness over the 'mato grosso' (jungle) beneath us, before a new day started in Brazil. During the flight, on-board personnel showed our children around the plane, including the cockpit where the door was left wide open. We could witness the children in the lap of the crew, watching the wall of instruments in a joint display of 'amisada'. Soon the message out of the cockpit reached us, "We have on board some new African 'imports'."

"The plane landed at night in an airport, which was way out of the city of Sao Paulo. To cover both eventualities of our arrival, our relatives from Brazil had split the party in two. One group was waiting at the 'Congonjas Airport' in Sao Paulo and the other one at 'Viracopos International Airport', two hundred kilometres outside of Sao Paulo. Heat, and an intensely aromatic atmosphere of the tropics, was our first welcome. Then came swarms of insects, swirling from outside, into the lights of the reception building. Large, deep sounding buzzing mixed with humming flies of various wing sizes.

"At the checkpoint, the party waiting at this airport took on the formalities for us to enter Brazil. Only local Brazilians knew the 'jeitinios' (assistance) of how to proceed straight through the control points. Besides other formalities, we also had to sign a document, according to which we had to produce all our fingerprints at an official police station. Were we moved in line with criminals? Anyway, life in Brazil

had taken off for us in Brazilian style. The welcome turned so much friendlier out past the checkpoints.

"The party in Sao Paulo heard about our arrival at the other airport and started on their way to join us all at their home in the countryside. The two Brazilian grandchildren were especially excited to 'have received these imports from Africa'. If it hadn't been for this friendly family reception in such different conditions to those in South Africa, not to mention Europe, I doubt we would have made this move. But now, having moved, it was up to us to build our lives in a very different country from what we'd seen so far."

Vinhedo, Brazil, 1975, family reunion

One step at the time was almost the rule in Brazil. The relatives' big house and surrounding property lay on a small hill-site with its own road leading through the property. A fence and a gate closer to the house divided the land into the housing and a small farming area. Space in the countryside of Brazil seemed to have little limitation compared to available spaces in Europe. South Africa could offer already a good deal in affordable spaces for a living. The settings on the property here in Brazil also included a nicely built cottage where our family took up residence without interfering in the daily lives of our relatives.

The children had so much new to discover, starting with the capybara pet (a Brazilian rodent from the jungle), citrus trees bearing fruit, Frangipani flowers, Poinsettia, Queen of the Night cacti, bamboo. All the while Martin prepared the steps outside for the family's own life. From the start, it was decided also in Brazil to stick to our concept of battling life by agreeing on division of tasks within the family. Arja was the 'Interior Minister', looking after 'home affairs' whereas Martin took on the position of 'external affairs'. Such careful division of tasks in daily life increases time available for the family.

In retrospect, our family made sure our lives ran steadily, with satisfaction and constant progress, even if it happened in small steps. The three years in Brazil gave us personal freedom to a degree that we had to stay alert to safety issues. It was important not to be in the wrong place at the wrong time, or be caught in the social upheavals of Brazil's society at the time. Brazil was still a military dictatorship, the leader ruling the country with an iron fist. Under its rule, foreign educated specialists enjoyed a good life in a growing economy.

Chacara Finlandia, Rua Flamboyantes, Varzea Paulista, Brazil

Banana harvest, Brazil

However, the vast majority of people in Brazil had a much lower living standard, which contributed to the social unrest in Brazil. 'Ordem e Progresso' (Order and Progress) was written as an icon on the Brazilian flag. When this was going to happen was not a real concern for Brazil's population because too many had never seen it and had believed 'blindly' in it for most of the time.

Brazilians like to take their time and what doesn't happen today, might happen tomorrow. No real concerns about that bothered them. The concern was that those who lived below the poverty line sometimes made daily life difficult. A vast majority of Brazilian people had to live with that situation and they rebelled from time to time. On the other hand, living comfortably amidst crying poverty didn't meld with our, Martin and Arja's way of thinking. It is just a matter of time before people are haunted by what is conveniently ignored.

People in Brazil have, however, made, and still make, big efforts to advance themselves. Everybody has to admit this if there is a fair account of the country and its people to be given. In reality however, this can only represent an individual shift of a notorious minority. Details to underpin these statements can be found in the biography of Martin and Arja, "Journey of a Lifetime, Volume 2."

After three years in Brazil, our family had done their best, working long, hard hours on the property, often under difficult climatic conditions. Our life in Brazil finally came down to this: the people were great; the conditions left plenty to wish for. After South Africa, Martin and Arja decided not to leave our children in such an uncertain future. It was a pity that the price for personal freedom in Brazil laid partly only within our own power but promised to catch up with us in the future. This situation was difficult to ignore if we were to know more than the current situation could tell.

The family in Brazil, 1976

Preparing leaving Brazil, 1977

Moving out of Brazil in late 1978 turned into a task beyond normal comprehension. Only endless determination led to our family touring South America in order to get out of Brazil. Experiencing South America as a whole at that time became just a little too adventurous to make the decision to call South America home. Most of the time, however, its people managed to deliver that spark of hope in a world they didn't otherwise know.

The 'unknown' caught up with the family on arrival in Venezuela. Here, the news about the move from South America to Canada was interrupted by social unrest in harbours across the Gulf of Mexico. Our plans ground to a halt. Such is life when a spirit of enterprise might turn against you. The remaining options returned Martin, Arja and our children to square one.

Not becoming idle meant moving back to better-known territory, even if it was only temporary. Questions of preference were at that moment not really the main concern, nor a priority. Finding a solution from where things could move on again, was the number one priority. Certainly, if one is not moving, one is spared finding new directions. On the other hand, experience shouldn't be underestimated as it always prepares one for the 'new'. Obviously, the inexperienced is more likely to remain disadvantaged.

In life, we can never know what lies ahead. Trying to avoid a move in life often merely postpones the changes to which one is asked to respond anyway. The details of how Martin, Arja, and our family came to leave Venezuela in forty-two degree Celsius heat and returned to Frankfurt in sub-zero temperatures can be found in Volume Two of their biography, "Journey of a Lifetime."

Albert Einstein already discovered: "Life is like riding a bicycle. To keep your balance you must keep moving."

CHAPTER 14

Excursion to Germany

The 'cold shower' effect of being back in 'Old-Germany', from where we had started, cooled the South American 'heat' for Martin, Arja and the children. We remembered, without having to ask questions, all the old well-known problems, albeit in a new modern edition. Already warning bells rang in our heads that we would not put up with this for long as we had picked up some useful comparisons along the way.

Bavaria-Germany, Tysse visit from Finland

Arja recalls her part in the move. "Well, to cut a long story short, I took the children to Finland, where we were more than welcome. No questions were asked while my husband Martin organized employment and a roof over our heads. What puzzled me was that when we had moved before, in the midst of a European winter during early 1979, our children had not complained. Now, on their own initiative, they began drawing comparisons with the richness of the tropics we had just left. Their constant cries were, "Why do we have to live in a country with such miserable cold weather and so many people?" This didn't take long to come to our attention.

"Almost three years were enough to ensure that we felt stuck in a 'rut' again. Pressure for progress in Germany still hadn't overcome the problems young families with children had in gaining even basic support. The younger generation had to compete for living situations with those who had 'made it', with or without children. Our German shepherd, for instance, found easier acceptance than our children in the search for a reasonable rented home. In addition, having the same people who rejected children as neighbours in your own flat or house didn't make for a desirable option.

"In a bottleneck with our rental situation, a change of scene seemed inevitably to become our solution. The hostilities surrounding our presence in an environment dominated by long established citizens didn't stop at our doorstep. It was mainly I who bore the brunt, as I was at home with the children day and night. For no obvious reason, locals made people like us feel insecure, not necessarily being carved out of the same 'local material' for long enough."

The family portrait, Germany, 1978

CHAPTER 15

Calling Australia Home

Frankfurt, departure to Australia, LH690, 1981

"Stern Magazine" reporting our departure
The family in Australia

It was mainly Arja feeling the stress this time. She wanted to make sure that the decision to move took into account all our past experiences. Moving from continent to continent with all the family's belongings did not exactly make for an easy job. This experience was not to be underestimated in the move to Australia, as far away as one could think of. Australia came to the party by approving our family's migration application. On hearing of that decision, many considered this win not much different from that of a lotto win.

Martin, Arja and the children struck it lucky again, setting foot in Australia, firstly in Melbourne. From then on, it was our choice where exactly to settle. The longest uninterrupted period in our family life started in Australia in 1981. This new country gave us the options to find a place to live, work and finally also to settle into after a comprehensive search for an ideal home.

Without previous experiences of other countries, it is doubtful that we could have held our ground at first, especially through the initial challenges migrants face in their first years in Australia. In Brazil especially, my family too had experienced how quickly cities can grow. People had no choice but to learn to put up with the increasingly dense living spaces. One could move again but this very quickly could become too expensive. Instead, our family decided to settle outside the city from the start. This became our answer as we searched for a place to settle. Fortunately, this proved to be the correct decision, at least up until now.

The cities started spreading out in Australia also, but fortunately not yet to the extent of other world mega-cities. Still the push continued with tightly competing conditions outside city boundaries. It all depends where one would like to live; either let the city catch up with you, or, you catch up with the city, but only when needed.

Twenty-five years later - since we bought land in a rural residential area – Martin and Arja know we could not afford to purchase even the land today. In Australia, it is plain to see that cities have pushed up prices far beyond the average person's financial feasibilities. Fortunately, despite all this city progress, the lifestyle on our rural residential property was left untouched.

Daughter Gucki and magpie, 1987

Years of work on the property created a family home we only could dream of before. Certainly, this was at a price of long, hard hours of work after a full day's work away from home. This included weekends as well, getting in as many hours as possible. 'Nothing has ever come from nothing' and therefore only unanimous perseverance of the family finally succeeded in our dream coming true. Our family had found far-reaching personal freedom in an environment in which we had worked hand in hand with nature.

Arja recalls her satisfaction at finally having a 'home'. "Our first building years were over. My husband Martin had performed all the tasks of the outside professional work and I had shouldered my share of work at home, including responding around the clock to the needs of our six children. This progress allowed us to reconnect to the family in Finland. After seven years in Australia, I caught the plane to Europe for the first time because of my mother's wish to come and see her again in Finland. At the stopover in Frankfurt, Germany, I just worked up the motivation to pay a limited visit to Martin's stepparents as well, who lived only a short distance further south.

"When we travel, we should always expect the unexpected. This caught up with me in Frankfurt on that first trip: the trains were on the verge of going on strike. For me, this meant having to keep my travel arrangements as short as possible in order not to miss my connection on my journey to Finland. Not far from the home of my parents-in-law, I had to use a taxi to cover the last leg as no train was running any more in the area.

"In the taxi, I spoke to the driver about the present traffic chaos. In return, the driver asked me, "Where do you come from?"

"I just arrived from Australia."

"Did you say from Australia? How did you come here?" He must have been confused with the local traffic situation, asking me such a question.

"I certainly did not arrive on foot."

"The next thing he asked was, "You are from Australia, but how come you speak fluent German?"

"When the taxi driver heard that I was shortly to go to Finland to my country of origin, he could not help shaking his head and cut short our conversation for the remainder of the trip. He probably was simply speechless, not knowing what else to say, after I had told him that in Australia more than seventy languages are spoken besides the official English. He was astounded that at home we speak both languages of our countries of origin besides the official one.

"My formal visit to Martin's parents' place was cut short to just a weekend until the train drivers' dispute could provide me with a passage back to Frankfurt Airport, from where I had booked my flight to Finland. Luck was on my side that at the same time the relatives from Brazil had also turned up on a visit, sparing me unnecessary questions about which I was a bit anxious. Instead, when my mother-in-law tried to enforce her viewpoint, I found smiling support from the Brazilian visitors' side. 'We both know her; it's her age. She doesn't mean it. Let's ignore what we don't like because we can afford to keep smiling. Tomorrow we'll be gone again.'"

"The 'Federal Garden Show' with its splendour, gave the visitors an excuse for a walk in and around the ancient town centre of Ettlingen. The centre shone with numerous, carefully exhibited flowerbeds alongside pebble-stone roads, lined with flower-decorated window fronts of solid-built, historical framework houses.

"My stay passed quickly and without fear of 'censure' thanks to the 'Brazilian' support. The farewell was also kind and swift, getting me on my next leg to Finland. On arrival in the capital Helsinki, our good Finnish friends from our time together in Heidelberg, Pirkko and Kalevi, welcomed me at the airport. Every time we arrived in Finland, alone or together, their warm welcome waited for us, never missing a farewell either. Time and distance often can show the real friends one has in life, not necessarily just those who are close by.

"In my home town of Turku, my mother and I couldn't wait to hug each other after my seven long years in faraway Australia. Mum did not want to let go of our embrace as if wanting to say, I am not letting you go any more. Nevertheless, a caring mum like mine knew that my home was with my family and where that family was, there too was my home.

"In later years during other visits back home in Finland, I experienced many strange face-to-face incidents when meeting other people. On one particular occasion, my mother took me out to a public performance in the open area of the city centre, where a group of young students from Lubeck in Germany sang in chorus German songs as well as Finnish ones. People gathering around the event clapped their hands in appreciation of the outstanding program. When I thanked them in German for their appearance, everybody's attention was directed to us. The conductor consequently came over, enquiring as to whether I came from Germany too, which I could only deny with a smile. Next, he saw the kangaroo-icon on my shirt, its home of Australia printed underneath in clear letters.

"You can't be from Australia either," was his next comment.

"Sorry to disappoint you, but I just arrived from there."

"Well you must therefore also speak English." On hearing only the word 'English', a gentleman next to me excitedly joined in our conversation, trying to throw in some poor sounding English words. He obviously had problems pronouncing the words properly.

"In order not to disappoint the gentleman in his efforts, I suggested, this time in Finnish, "Why are we taking the difficult road in a conversation when we are all calling Finland our home?" The gentleman shaking his head in obvious disbelief, had only this to say, "I don't know any more in what world we are living. Who could say where somebody comes from today?"

"After that, I was in something of a quandary, not knowing what to say in return. Gaining back my confidence in a hurry, I added that I was from Finland, my husband hailed from Romania but was brought up in Germany, and we live with our family in Australia.

"Aha, this is why!" echoed from around me. As far as I was concerned, I realized that it was not always easy keeping a conversation simple when people from different background meet. In the end however, everybody was pleased to have understood each other thanks to my various language-bridging skills, which finally did make things easier. Mum was so proud that somebody from the family in Finland could converse so obviously with people from other countries.

"This you learn best by living with people in their country," has become my experience.

"My stay in Finland passed fleetingly, daily visiting other family members, neighbours and school acquaintances, preferably not too far from my mother's place. Here I spent most of the time with her trying to convince her to join me on the way back home to Australia. In her imagination, Australia was worlds away from Finland. However, most of all, her generation could not travel to other countries, especially to distant ones in other continents, or learn foreign languages. This time around, I had to be content with leaving her behind in Finland until another time.

"During my absence from Australia, I lost the connection to my family as nobody answered the phone. This was only a few days before my departure from Finland. Terrible fears of the house having burnt to the ground constantly returned to haunt me until I took the initiative, calling upon friends at home in Australia. They turned up at our place, reporting that everything was right as rain except the phone connection was playing up again. Even though my strong affection for my mother couldn't be denied, nothing could keep me in Finland much longer. From that moment, a strong desire caught up with me to be reunited with my family. Distance can have a magical force upon one's own longings, testing them thoroughly.

"Arriving back in Australia, now, as well as in coming years, amounted to a new start within an existing direction in our lives. Only when leaving daily routines, can one realize where we have gone and most of all that we have imperceptibly changed. At the time of my first coming home to Australia, it was instrumental in continuing on the path that we've found ourselves in a new country like Australia.

"Living in a warm climate made daily life so much easier. Where we live, on the doorsteps to the tropics, neither clothing nor heating was an issue. Shorts and a t-shirt were sufficient for almost the entire year around and the sun-hat easily took the place of a winter fur-cap.

"In 1992, I finally managed to bring my mother all the way from Finland to our home in Australia. For her part, this was indeed a courageous move, not only in respect to her age of seventy-five, but more so with regard to the long distance to Australia. Even ten years later, she had the courage to take this step again and see our family in Australia for the last time. I still remember her excitement when she exclaimed shortly after leaving Helsinki by air for London, "How soon will we arrive in Australia?" After barely two hours of travelling to London, I comforted my mum that the big journey was soon to start in London.

"Both times on her way to Australia, Mum felt herself transferred into another world, especially when she arrived in the southern hemisphere winter, where in our place it was warmer than in the summer in Finland. In our environment, there was definitely no snow to been seen. Rather a multitude of flowers on bushes and trees benefited from the intense winter sun and its dry resting time. On arriving at our place, mum's message was a joyful one, "This must be paradise! Everything, the trees, flowers, even the house look so much more beautiful than the pictures you sent over the years." It was only during some nights when the temperature difference between daytime, hovering around twenty-five degree Celsius, and dropping occasionally at night to less than ten degree Celsius, were we reminded briefly of a colder winter. The early morning hours however, pushed aside this memory very quickly with a rising, fiery morning sun.

"We were left with strong memories of Mum when I returned her personally to Finland after three months with us. Her only complaint was that our children didn't speak the Finnish language. One might have thought that we had abandoned our language heritage, but it was the children who didn't want to speak Finnish at least at home any more after a number of years away from direct contact with Finland. To accommodate everybody has always been impossible. The conclusion was inevitably that, as long as we aim for the better, we have a chance of satisfying the majority of people as well as ourselves.

"Also, my mum took back so many good memories that she could go on her 'last journey' back to Finland, in peace, after leaving us for the second and last time. To continue with our lives, whether in Finland or Australia, has always been, and still is, the best thing to do in order to pay homage to loved ones."

Arja and Martin, Bribie Island, Qld., 1997

EPILOGUE

And that was it!

In *A Wild Herb Soup* Emilie Carles writes, "I believe most of us have locked away episodes that one may not wish to recall, but which nevertheless should be exposed so that others may learn that life does not always run on an even keel. There are many ups and downs, like the ebb and flow of the sea, and it is amazing sometimes how one can derive strength and a will to survive when one's spirit seems to hover at the lowest ebb."

Arja's life's journey can be seen as two distinct periods. The first leg principally is this story, which leads on to the second leg - a much bigger journey side by side with her own family. The interesting part of those two journeys is in the different starting points of the main 'actors', Arja and her husband, Martin. Geographical differences as well as ethnic differences were part of life's unpredictable courses.

Arja recalls the foundation of her life, "To begin with, my life, which hails from a stable and happy youth in Finland, moved into the relatively unknown territory of a life so much different from my original one. It raises, in hindsight, questions as to whether or not individuals can answer life's challenges better from a similar or different background. In a world of constant changes on the increase, it looks more likely that the ones who move with those demands, regardless of their background, have better chances to succeed in life. Whereas to continue the convention into which one was born, as was more or less the custom, should be a thing of the past. Instead, listening today to different opinions has become the priority.

"We can only learn from others to avoid life in isolation. In addition, I went out of the home-security into the world to find a life of new challenges, which in return have built on strength and will, for a better survival. People would go to any length during their lives to achieve something, but the real starting point to it would be in preparing ourselves first and then going out to find a friend, a partner, a husband with whom challenges can be shared for the benefit of both and not just for one."

Thus opens a path for more people around us to share in efforts for common goals. We are also not supposed to become lonely travellers. Rather we should be " like a wine on its way to maturity with the help of others, it gets better and more interesting as one awakens memories and brings forth that is significant in one's life and perhaps passes over that which is not" as Emilie Carles describes our life journey.

This is what I had in mind with documenting the first leg of my life's journey and adding my own viewpoints to it. I have been in the lucky company of courage, which helped to successfully make first my own life-journey and then the other journey jointly with loved ones, friends and acquaintances. The second, more significant leg, is documented in "Journey of a Lifetime, Volume two". Volume one tells my husband's story of the first leg of his journey."